BRINGING DOWN A PRESIDENT

BRINGING DOWN A PRESIDENT

THE WATERGATE SCANDAL

ANDREA BALIS & ELIZABETH LEVY

ILLUSTRATIONS BY **TIM FOLEY**

ROARING BROOK PRESS
NEW YORK

Published by Roaring Brook Press
Roaring Brook Press is a division of Holtzbrinck Publishing Holdings Limited Partnership
120 Broadway, New York, NY 10271
mackids.com

Library of Congress Cataloging-in-Publication Data is available.
ISBN 978-1-250-17679-0

Our books may be purchased in bulk for promotional, educational, or business use. Please
contact your local bookseller or the Macmillan Corporate and Premium Sales Department
at (800) 221-7945 ext. 5442 or by email at MacmillanSpecialMarkets@macmillan.com.

First edition, 2019
Book design by April Ward

Printed in the United States of America by LSC Communications,
Harrisonburg, Virginia

1   3   5   7   9   10   8   6   4   2

TO EACH OTHER

WHEN THE PRESIDENT DOES IT, THAT MEANS THAT IT IS NOT ILLEGAL.

—RICHARD NIXON

CONTENTS

PART THREE: THE GREAT UNRAVELING

CAST OF LEADING CHARACTERS

THE PRESIDENT

Richard Nixon: Thirty-seventh president of the United States

HIS TEAM

Alexander Butterfield: Deputy assistant to the president, Haldeman's aide

Charles (Chuck) Colson: Special counsel to the president

John Dean: Counsel to the president

John Ehrlichman: Assistant to the president for domestic affairs

JOHN DEAN

JOHN EHRLICHMAN

H. R. (Bob) Haldeman: White House chief of staff

Herb Kalmbach: Nixon's personal attorney, campaign fund-raiser

Jeb Magruder: Deputy director of the Committee to Re-Elect the President

BOB HALDEMAN

John Mitchell: U.S. attorney general (1969–1972)

Anthony "Tony U." Ulasewicz: Ex–New York City police officer, in charge of payoffs to burglars

JOHN MITCHELL

THE PLUMBERS/ BURGLARS
THE HONCHOS

E. Howard Hunt: Retired CIA agent

G. Gordon Liddy: Retired FBI agent

James McCord: Retired CIA agent

E. HOWARD HUNT

THE BURGLARS FROM CUBA (VIA MIAMI)

Bernard Barker

Virgilio Gonzalez

G. GORDON LIDDY

BRINGING DOWN A PRESIDENT

JAMES McCORD

Eugenio Martínez

Frank Sturgis

THE PROSECUTORS

Archibald Cox: Watergate special prosecutor

Leon Jaworski: Watergate special prosecutor

Elliot Richardson: U.S. attorney general (1973)

THE CONGRESSIONAL TEAM

Sam Dash: Chief counsel of the Ervin Committee

Sam Ervin: Chairman of the Senate Select Committee on Presidential Campaign Activities (the Ervin Committee)

Peter Rodino: Chairman of the House Judiciary Committee

THE NEWSPAPER TEAM

CARL BERNSTEIN

BOB WOODWARD

Carl Bernstein: Reporter for the *Washington Post*

Ben Bradlee: Executive editor of the *Washington Post*

Bob Woodward: Reporter for the *Washington Post*

INTRODUCTION

The Watergate, in Washington, D.C., is a shining white complex of apartments, offices, and a hotel with balconies that look like sharks' teeth. If you are ever visiting the nation's capital, you and your family can stay in the hotel. In 1972, Watergate was the site of the most famous burglary in U.S. history. And a very weird burglary it was: Nothing was stolen. The burglars wore suits and ties, and blue plastic gloves. They carried crisp one-hundred-dollar bills into the burglary site. But the thing that made this burglary so famous is the fact that the burglars worked for the president of the United States.

Mary McCarthy (a journalist and Watergate resident): It is very different today when tourists roam through the lobby buying Watergate joke material, including bugs, at the newsstand.

Today the word "gate" gets attached to scandals around the world. But Watergate is where it all began.

When people hear about scandals, they often say, "I wish I had been a fly on the wall." They mean they wish they could know every word that was actually said. Real flies have eyes that help them see in every direction at once. In our book, the Fly on the Wall is your narrator.

Reading the actual words of the players in this scandal reminds us that these were real people, in real situations, and they did not know how it would end. For many of them, it ended in a jail cell.

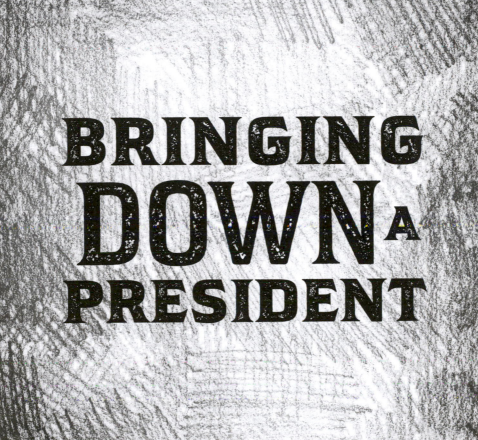

BRINGING DOWN A PRESIDENT

PART ONE

THE GAME BEGINS

HE'D NEVER BE
ABLE TO OPERATE THE
BUGGING EQUIPMENT
ON HIS OWN.

—JOHN EHRLICHMAN

TO BE A FLY ON THE WALL

FLY ON THE WALL: It is hard to say when a historical event begins, but one place to start the story of Watergate might be February 16, 1971. On that day, President Richard M. Nixon and his faithful aide Alexander Butterfield stood by the president's desk in the Oval Office. They were staring at the new, up-to-date recording device that the Secret Service had installed at the president's request and hidden under his desk.

Nixon (turning solemnly to Butterfield): Mum's the word.

FLY ON THE WALL: Some leaders, such as pharaohs and kings, have built pyramids or monuments so history will remember them. Nixon got a monument of his own words. He wanted a record of everything that was said in the Oval Office. According

to H. R. (Bob) Haldeman, Nixon's chief of staff, the president wanted to use that record to write his own history.

Haldeman (looking back on Watergate): Nixon and I agreed something had to be done to ensure that we possessed an accurate record of what was said . . . for his eventual memoirs.

FLY ON THE WALL: Nixon didn't want anyone except a few people on his staff to know about the devices recording thousands of hours of conversations—3,700 hours, to be exact. There's so much tape that the recordings are still being transcribed to this day. There were seven microphones in the Oval Office: five in Nixon's desk alone and one on each side of the fireplace. Dozens more were scattered around wherever Nixon might go. All of these microphones were hooked up to recorders hidden in a White House locker room that nobody used anymore. Almost every single word that Nixon or anybody else said in the Oval Office, including each phone conversation, would be recorded day and night. And everybody, especially a president, says things they don't want certain other people to hear.

> **Haldeman:** Mr. President, you'll never remember to turn it on except when you don't want it, and when you do want it, you're always going to be shouting.

FLY ON THE WALL: Other modern presidents before Nixon had also had taping systems in the Oval Office. The two previous presidents, John F. Kennedy and Lyndon B. Johnson, could turn their voice-recording devices on and off whenever they wanted to. But Nixon's aides, including top aide John Ehrlichman, were afraid that the president wouldn't be able to handle that kind of system. Nixon was a physically awkward human being. At award ceremonies during his presidency, he dropped so many medals (or accidentally stabbed the recipients) that his staff had to retrofit all ceremonial medals, like the Medal of Honor, to make them clip-ons.

> **Ehrlichman:** We knew he'd never be able to operate the bugging equipment on his own.

THE GANG THAT COULDN'T BURGLE STRAIGHT

I don't think I had ever seen middle-aged burglars in suits and ties. It was bizarre.

—Police sergeant Paul Leeper, who arrested the Watergate burglars

FLY ON THE WALL: Richard Nixon, a Republican, had been elected president of the United States in 1968; four years later, in 1972, he was running for reelection. That year, on May 25, a team of henchmen working for the White House gathered at the Watergate Hotel to break into the headquarters of the Democratic National Committee (DNC), located on the sixth floor. They were especially interested in bugging the phone of Larry O'Brien, head of the DNC. Their plan was to rent a banquet room at the Watergate Hotel, sneak up the stairs to the offices of the people in charge of the Democratic campaign for president—Nixon's rivals—and bug their phones. As long as they had to be in the banquet room (which they'd rented for only a few hours), they decided to have a fine lobster dinner with a nice selection of wines.

Security guard (poking his head in at the end of his shift): Your rental time is up.

FLY ON THE WALL: The men made a big fuss as they got ready to leave. During the confusion, two of the men—E. Howard Hunt and G. Gordon Liddy (who'd planned the operation)—hid in a closet. They planned to wait until the hotel went quiet before sneaking up the stairs. In the middle of the night, they tried to leave the closet, only to discover that they were locked in. They had to wait until the cleaning crew came in the morning to let them out.

Hunt: Gordon, I know you like scotch, but don't ever drink it at the Watergate Hotel.

Liddy: Why not?

Hunt: Because last night in that damn closet, I had to take a leak in the worst way. I was desperate. I finally found a nearly empty bottle of Johnnie Walker Red. It's quite full now.

Liddy: Ah, I can see Larry O'Brien now with a puzzled look on his face, saying, "Funny, if I didn't know this was scotch, I'd swear it was piss."

FLY ON THE WALL: The determined burglars didn't give up. They tried again after two days, and this time they got in and placed their listening devices. Later, they found out that one of the bugs didn't work—maybe it was broken, or maybe it was the installation. A few weeks later, they tried again. They rented two rooms at the hotel. They also took a room across the street at the Howard Johnson Motel in order to have a lookout.

This time they relied on room service for their meal, and they avoided the closets. At 12:45 A.M. on June 17, the burglars moved into the stairwell of the Watergate. James McCord, a former agent with the Central Intelligence Agency (CIA), used masking tape to hold open the latches of the sixth-, eighth-, and ninth-floor stairwell doors—just to be sure the burglars wouldn't lock themselves out. Unfortunately, he placed the tape horizontally across the latches, instead of vertically, which would have hidden it. A security guard named Frank Wills saw the masking tape. He took it off, thinking it had been left by the cleaning crew, and went on his scheduled break.

A few minutes later, when the burglars checked to make sure one of the doors was open, the tape was gone. So they replaced it.

A big mistake.

When Frank Wills came back from his break, he saw that the tape had reappeared. It made him suspicious.

Wills (in 911 call to police): There's a burglary in progress at the Watergate.

FLY ON THE WALL: Upstairs, unaware that the cops had been called, the burglars couldn't pick the lock to the DNC office, so they decided to completely remove the door. They heard footsteps in the stairwell and got worried, but now that the door was off its hinges, they were committed. They turned off their walkie-talkies so nobody would hear them.

Another mistake, as noted by police sergeant Paul Leeper.

Leeper: We didn't jump out of the car and go running up there. You get so many calls like that—"burglary in progress"—and 95 percent of them aren't worth anything.

FLY ON THE WALL: The fact that the burglary was at the posh Watergate Hotel, however, made the police decide to check it out. When the lookout across the street at the Howard Johnson saw some unknown men, he called Liddy and Hunt, the two in charge in the room they had rented at the hotel. The lookout wasn't sure at first that the men were cops; Leeper was working undercover in his usual disguise—that of a hippie—which he often wore to blend in with drug dealers or political protesters. He was accompanied by Officer John Barrett.

Lookout: Hey, any of our guys wearing hippie clothes?

Liddy: Negative. All of our men are in business suits. Why?

Lookout: They're on the sixth floor now. One's got on a cowboy hat. One's got on a sweatshirt. It looks like . . . guns . . . guns . . . They've got guns. . . . It's trouble.

Liddy: [Expletive deleted] . . . Hunt and I realized that something was very wrong.

Barrett (shouting): Police! Come out with your hands up.

Wills: Five middle-aged guys stand up. They were wearing suits and ties and blue surgical gloves, and they had walkie-talkies and all this electrical stuff.

FLY ON THE WALL: The cops ordered the five burglars to face the wall. The cops were nervous because they had only two pairs of handcuffs between them, and there were five burglars.

Wills: Officer Barrett eyed one man with a black overnight bag in one hand and a trench coat draped over the other. Barrett yelled again, to raise his hands, and the man didn't move. Barrett aimed his pistol at the man's chest. Another man said something in Spanish, and his hands flew up.

Leeper (patting down the men): I found penlights, tiny tear gas canisters, the keys to Room 214 at the Watergate, and a spiral notebook with a key taped to the cover. I don't think I had ever seen middle-aged burglars in suits and ties. It was bizarre.

FLY ON THE WALL: The burglars were carrying a stack of crisp, sequentially numbered hundred-dollar bills. This was not something the cops were used to finding on burglars. Usually burglars take money—they don't arrive with it. When asked their names, the burglars gave fake identities. Unfortunately, two of them picked the same name.

> **Barrett:** I said, "Wait a minute, fellow, you've got to get your stories straight," and they giggled.

FLY ON THE WALL: While the burglars in the Watergate building had their hands up, Liddy and Hunt, who had arrived at the Howard Johnson lookout room, knew they were in trouble.

> **Liddy:** We began packing everything of an incriminating nature that we could find. Howard slipped an antenna down his pants leg, which gave him a stiff-legged gait. We walked out. The place was swarming with police and squad cars.

FLY ON THE WALL: When Liddy got home, his wife woke up and asked if anything was wrong.

> **Liddy:** There was trouble. Some people got caught. I'll probably be going to jail.

FLY ON THE WALL: He would go to jail, and so would the burglars he had abandoned at the Watergate. When the police checked the burglars' pockets, they discovered that the cash wasn't all they were carrying. They had an address book that included the White House telephone number. Officers Leeper and Barrett called in the Federal Bureau of Investigation (FBI). The Watergate scandal had begun.

The morning after the break-in, the five Watergate burglars—McCord, along with four men who lived in Miami and had ties to Cuba (Virgilio Gonzalez, Eugenio Martínez, Frank Sturgis, and CIA agent Bernard Barker)—appeared in court before Judge James Belson. The government, represented by prosecutor Earl J. Silbert, presented its case against the Watergate burglars. People called Silbert "Earl the Pearl" for the courtroom entertainment he provided.

> **Silbert (to Judge Belson):** They should not be released on bond. They have given false names, have not cooperated with the police, possessed $2,300 in cash, and have a tendency to travel abroad. They have been arrested in a "professional burglary" with a "clan . . . des . . . tine" purpose.
>
> **Belson:** What are your professions?
>
> **Barker:** Anti-communist.

FLY ON THE WALL: The other burglars nodded.

> **Belson (beckoning McCord to step forward):** Your occupation?
>
> **McCord:** Security consultant.
>
> **Belson:** Where?

McCord (softly): I've recently retired from government service.

Belson (loudly): Where in government?

McCord (in a whisper): CIA.

FLY ON THE WALL: Bob Woodward, a twenty-nine-year-old reporter from the *Washington Post*, was sitting in the courtroom. He leaned forward.

FLY ON THE WALL: At the time of the break-in, Nixon was relaxing in Florida. He did read a small article in the *Miami Herald*:

MIAMIANS HELD IN D.C. TRY TO BUG DEMO HEADQUARTERS

Nixon: I dismissed it as some sort of a prank.

FLY ON THE WALL: Still, Nixon was worried. The first person he called was an old friend named Charles (Chuck) Colson, who served as special counsel to the president, meaning he advised the president on legal matters related to the administration.

> ***Time* magazine:** Of all the sordid Watergate cast, Charles Colson was widely viewed in Washington as the wiliest, slickest operator and thus the least likely to be charged with a crime.

FLY ON THE WALL: Colson acted as Nixon's "hatchet man"—a person hired to carry out disagreeable or underhanded tasks. His attitude might have been summed up by a sign he had on a wall in his house:

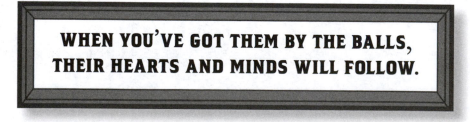

WHEN YOU'VE GOT THEM BY THE BALLS, THEIR HEARTS AND MINDS WILL FOLLOW.

Nixon (to Colson about the Watergate scandal): This is not one that is going to get people excited because they don't give a sh*t about repression and bugging and all the rest.

Colson: I think they expect it. . . . They think that political parties do this all the time.

Nixon: They certainly do.

FLY ON THE WALL: This was—and still is—a big problem. When people assume their political parties are corrupt, and when they worry about their own government eavesdropping on them, then if that society happens to be a democracy, the whole system falls apart. Democracy demands trust in the government's essential honesty. But that didn't seem to matter to Nixon.

THE PLUMBERS

Since my will was now so strong, I could endure a long, deep, flesh-charring burn without a flicker of expression.

—G. Gordon Liddy

FLY ON THE WALL: Leaks from the White House to the press were nothing new; even George Washington complained about them.

I am much inflamed. But if freedom of speech is taken away, then dumb and silent we may be led like sheep to the slaughter.

FLY ON THE WALL: Richard Nixon did not care about freedom of the press (enshrined in the First Amendment to the U.S. Constitution) and was paranoid that details about his administration would be leaked to reporters who would make damaging information public. On June 24, 1971, he created the secret Special Investigations Unit to hunt down anyone who did the leaking. On this unit he had two trusted aides in particular. One of them was his chief of staff, Bob Haldeman, a Californian who somehow kept his tan year-round. Haldeman did everything from checking to see that the cottage cheese arrived weekly from Nixon's favorite dairy in Los Angeles to making sure that nobody got in to see Nixon without his say-so.

> **Haldeman:** Every President needs a son of a bitch, and I'm Nixon's. I'm his buffer and his bastard. I get done what he wants done, and I take the heat instead of him.

FLY ON THE WALL: John Ehrlichman, assistant to the president for domestic affairs, was another Californian in the Special Investigations Unit. He and Haldeman had identical buzz cuts, and they both knew that their boss's moods could get them in trouble. They knew that Nixon's desire to defeat his enemies could lead him into complicated plots to get revenge. And they knew that some of these activities would be illegal.

> **Nixon (after resigning in disgrace):** Well, when the president does it, that means that it is not illegal.

FLY ON THE WALL: That's not true. Nobody is above the law, not even the president. That was the whole point of the

American Revolution: The country is ruled by laws, not by a king. Nixon wasn't the only person who forgot that—so did the men around him. To protect the president, Haldeman and Ehrlichman began to carry out dirty tricks. They found themselves a clever aide, David Young, and put him in charge of the Special Investigations Unit. They gave Young his own freshly painted new office (Room 16, on the ground floor of the old Executive Office Building), his own telephone scrambler, a three-way combination safe, and a secretary.

> **Young (in a television interview):** I was talking to my mother-in-law, who asked, "What are you working on, dear?" I told her, "I am plugging leaks." She said, "Oh, how nice. We had a carpenter in the family, and now we have a plumber."

FLY ON THE WALL: Thus, the president's men were known thereafter as "the plumbers." Young liked the word "plumber" so much that he hung a sign on his door: MR. YOUNG: PLUMBER. One of the earliest plumbers was G. Gordon Liddy, a former FBI agent and a strange man. Liddy was inordinately proud of showing off his determination. He had developed a personal ritual that he called "building my willpower." The ritual involved scorching his left hand and forearm in flames. He used his left hand because his right hand was his gun hand. He loved guns. Liddy progressed from burning himself with cigarettes to testing himself with candles.

> **Liddy:** Since my will was now so strong, I could endure

a long, deep, flesh-charring burn without a flicker of expression.

FLY ON THE WALL: Liddy once tried to recruit a young woman named Sherry Stevens to work as secretary for the plumbers. She was scared that she could get in trouble.

Stevens: I'm worried. They can make anybody talk.

Liddy: Nobody will know.

Stevens: But you will know.

Liddy: Nobody can make me talk. Just hold your cigarette lighter and turn it on me.

FLY ON THE WALL: Stevens did as Liddy asked. While he held his left palm over the flame, he looked into Stevens's eyes. His ability to do that frightened her. She decided not to take the job, opting out by using a fact from her personal life as an excuse.

Stevens: I know you would never betray me, but I just remembered that in September, I'm going to marry a Swiss airplane pilot.

FLY ON THE WALL: Liddy's boss was John Mitchell, Nixon's attorney general. Mitchell was a New Yorker, and he was one of the many father figures Nixon seemed to want around him. Mitchell was one of the few people whom Nixon considered his equal.

Nixon (speaking of Mitchell): I have found my heavyweight.

FLY ON THE WALL: In private, Mitchell did not respect Nixon as much as Nixon thought.

Mitchell: Nixon couldn't piss straight in the shower if I wasn't there to hold him.

FLY ON THE WALL: Guess where the attorney general and his wife, Martha, lived? That's right: the Watergate Hotel.

Authors Madeleine Edmondson and Alden Duer Cohen (writing of Martha Mitchell): From the beginning she was the darling of the press, with her Southern charm. She adored dressing up and speaking her mind.

FLY ON THE WALL: The Nixon administration was tickled at first by Martha's popularity. She made them seem more human. She became the first cabinet wife to be assigned a press secretary, and the TV cameras loved her. But sometimes, especially after Martha drank, she could be a little too honest.

Martha Mitchell: I love to wind my tongue up and I love to make it go.

FLY ON THE WALL: Nixon, however, figured that Martha was John's problem. The president didn't trust his own political party—he needed John. He set up a separate campaign committee in 1970 and appointed John Mitchell to head it. Officially it was called the Committee to Re-Elect the President (CRP), but everyone, even the people who worked there, called it CREEP.

John Mitchell was perfect for his job, even if Martha didn't think so.

Martha Mitchell: Quitting the Justice Department in favor of CREEP is a very bad move . . . that just breaks my heart.

FLY ON THE WALL: Mitchell didn't take his wife's broken heart into account. Part of his job as the head of CREEP was to coordinate with the plumbers. The head plumber, Liddy, had big plans.

Liddy (writing later in his memoir): We had a meeting with John Mitchell. We presented our plan for clandestine entries, or "black bag jobs."

FLY ON THE WALL: On January 27, 1972, Liddy hatched Operation Gemstone to carry out these "black bag jobs," a name for breaking-and-entering activities meant to gather information. Mitchell listened to Liddy's plan.

Liddy: [We can] identify the leaders of "disturbances." We could kidnap them, drug them, and hold them in Mexico until after the Republican convention, then release them unharmed, still wondering what happened.

FLY ON THE WALL: As Liddy said that his budget for the plan would be $1 million, Mitchell puffed on his pipe. People don't smoke pipes much anymore, but there's a lot of fussing with a pipe. If you're talking to someone with a pipe, he might look serious, and you have to wait for him to speak while he puffs on the stem and tamps down the tobacco.

Mitchell (filling and relighting his pipe): Gordon, a million dollars is a hell of a lot of money, much more than we had in mind. I'd like you to come back with something more realistic. And Gordon . . .

Liddy: Yes, sir?

Mitchell: Burn those charts. Do it personally.

Liddy: Yes, sir.

FLY ON THE WALL: Liddy was forced to settle for a budget of a half million dollars. That was the money that paid for the burglary at the Watergate. The idea for the break-in came about because Nixon wanted to know everything the head of the Democratic National Committee, Larry O'Brien, was doing.

Mitchell's deputy and right-hand man at CREEP, Jeb Magruder, met with Liddy to review Liddy's plans.

Magruder: Gordon, do you think you can get into the Watergate?

Liddy: Yes, it's a high-security building, but we can do it.

Magruder: How about putting a bug in O'Brien's office?

Liddy: All right, we can do it. The phones too?

Magruder: And while you're in there, photograph whatever you find.

FLY ON THE WALL: When Magruder looked back on this, he admitted that these acts he was casually asking for were illegal.

Magruder: Although I was aware . . . they were illegal and I'm sure the others did, we had become [used] to using some activities that would help us [in] accomplishing what we thought was a cause, a legitimate cause.

FLY ON THE WALL: So that's how on June 17, 1972, Gordon Liddy and Howard Hunt came to be hiding in the Howard Johnson Motel while James McCord and the four other burglars were caught red-handed and bewildered in their business suits and rubber gloves, carrying wiretapping devices and all those crisp hundred-dollar bills.

A SMOKING GUN

It's a third-rate burglary attempt.
—Ron Ziegler, Nixon's press secretary, June 18, 1972

**We were pleased that the *Post* carried only
a brief story by two reporters we had never heard
of, Carl Bernstein and Bob Woodward.**
—G. Gordon Liddy

Richard Nixon (on June 20, 1972): It's fortunately a
bizarre story.

Bob Haldeman: Yeah.

Nixon: Don't you think so?

Haldeman: Its bizarreness almost helps to discredit it.

FLY ON THE WALL: The best way to discredit the burglary was to blame it on somebody—and Haldeman came up with the perfect fall guy.

Haldeman: The plan is this guy Liddy . . . confessing . . .

Nixon: Liddy?

Haldeman: Nobody pays attention to him.

Nixon: Who's he? He's the guy with the detective agency?

Haldeman: No. . . . Apparently, he is a little bit nuts. He sort of likes the dramatic. He's said, "If you want to put me before a firing squad and shoot me, that's fine. I'd like to be like Nathan Hale."

FLY ON THE WALL: Nathan Hale, by the way, was a twenty-one-year-old spy for the Americans during the Revolutionary War. The British caught him and hanged him in 1776. According to legend, his final words were:

I only regret that I have but one life to lose for my country.

FLY ON THE WALL: Hale became a hero because somebody wrote down what he said. Haldeman's and Nixon's words have been preserved, too—via the recording devices Nixon placed in the Oval Office—but they aren't quite so heroic.

> **Haldeman (on June 23, 1972):** Now, on the investigation . . . the FBI is not under control, the way to handle this now is for us to have the CIA . . . call the FBI [and] just say, stay the hell out of this business here, we don't want you to go any further.

> **Nixon:** Good deal. Play it tough. That's the way they play it, and that's the way we are going to play it.

FLY ON THE WALL: In case you weren't paying attention, Nixon had just approved a plan to ask the CIA to lie to the FBI. This is what is known as "criminal conspiracy to obstruct justice," which means making a plan with someone else to interfere with a legal process. And the White House tapes were spinning.

> **Jeb Magruder:** The basic goal of the cover story was to make Liddy solely responsible for the break-ins. I was the next line of defense after Liddy. We were not covering up a burglary. We were safeguarding world peace.

FLY ON THE WALL: No, they weren't. They were covering their own asses. And their attempt to cover up the Watergate break-in was about to come back to bite them.

INSIDE NIXON'S HEAD

FLY ON THE WALL: Richard Nixon grew up poor in Yorba Linda, California—the edge of America. When Nixon was born, there were fewer than three hundred people in town.

Nixon: [My father] had a lemon ranch. It was the poorest lemon ranch in California, I can assure you.

FLY ON THE WALL: A railroad track ran through the town, and the Nixons lived on the "wrong" side. His father never made it out of sixth grade and had a very bad temper. His mother, Hannah Milhous Nixon, had more education, but in 1913, the year Nixon was born, women weren't allowed to vote, no matter how long they had gone to school.

Even when Nixon was a little kid, he was different. He dressed very neatly in starched white shirts. Sometimes, he would carry his shoes in a bag so they wouldn't get dusty.

Nixon's mother, Hannah Nixon: He was very fussy, always neat.

FLY ON THE WALL: In 1920, when he was in just second grade, Nixon started telling his classmates who he thought their parents should vote for in the upcoming presidential election. His choice was Warren G. Harding, the Republican candidate. The seven-year-old Nixon's adult-like seriousness did not make him popular. Many years later, Henry Kissinger, who served as Nixon's secretary of state, looked back on Nixon's career and thought about his personal history.

> **Kissinger:** Can you imagine what this man would have been like if somebody had loved him?

FLY ON THE WALL: In high school, Nixon tried out for the Latin Club's play and got the lead only because he had the highest scores in Latin. Onstage, he had to take a girl named Ola Florence Welch in his arms. His embrace was so awkward that the audience hooted and booed.

> **Nixon:** The hour on stage was agony beyond belief and almost beyond endurance. . . . An unbelievably horrendous experience.

Florence Welch (in her diary): Oh how I hate Richard Nixon. We never practiced it. . . . The kids went to pieces. I just about died.

FLY ON THE WALL: If there is one thing that is true about Richard Nixon, both as a boy and later as a man, it is that you could knock him down, but despite his awkwardness, he'd get right back up. He never seemed to accept defeat. He lost many elections, but it never stopped him. And he showed the same persistence when it came to getting the girl he wanted: The girl he had embraced in the play, Ola Florence Welch, eventually became his girlfriend.

Welch: [My friends asked me] how I could abide such a "stuffy" boyfriend. . . . I thought Dick was wonderful. . . . He wrote me notes which I just couldn't believe, they had such beautiful words. . . . We had a stormy relationship, more stormy than most. . . . Sometimes he'd be harsh and I'd cry. Then we'd make up.

FLY ON THE WALL: Nixon knew that education was the way out of Yorba Linda—and away from all those kids who made fun of him. He needed to prove that he was really someone. He won a full scholarship to Harvard but couldn't go because he didn't have the money for the train fare. Instead, Nixon ended up going to nearby Whittier College. When the most popular club on campus, the Franklins, turned him down, he started his own club. He gave it a fake Greek name, Orthogonians, which he said meant "straight shooters." He was the club's first president.

Nixon: They [the Franklins] were the haves. We were the have-nots. We were officially dedicated to what we called the four Bs: Beans, Brawn, Brain, and Bowels.

FLY ON THE WALL: "Beans" stood for energy, and "bowels" stood for guts. Nixon certainly didn't lack for guts. He tried out for football, even though he weighed only 145 pounds.

Nixon's college coach: We used him as a punching bag. Anyone who could take the beating he had to take was brave.

FLY ON THE WALL: Nixon may have lacked brawn, but beans, brain, and bowels finally did get him a ticket on a train to Duke Law School, in Durham, North Carolina, where he won yet another full scholarship. He shared his dreams with Welch— to become chief justice of the Supreme Court.

Welch: I always thought he would achieve something extraordinary in life, [although] never in my wildest dreams did I ever picture him as President of the United States.

FLY ON THE WALL: Nixon graduated from law school near the top of his class, but when he applied for jobs at the best law firms in New York City, he was rejected. And as always when he was rejected, he resented it.

Nixon: I knew these firms hired only from . . . the Ivy League Law schools. . . . I must have looked pretty scruffy sitting in those plush polished mahogany and leather reception rooms in my one good suit.

FLY ON THE WALL: Duke law degree in hand, Nixon went back home to California, where he met his future wife, Pat Ryan, whom other students called "quite a dish." They met at an audition for a community play.

Nixon (in his memoir): I could not take my eyes away from her. For me, it was a case of love at first sight.

FLY ON THE WALL: Not so much for Pat. She kept putting him off. Nixon kept trying.

Nixon (in a love letter to Pat): I am certainly not the Romeo type. I may not say much when I am with you—but all of me loves you all the time.

FLY ON THE WALL: Finally, Nixon presented Pat with a ring in a little box of flowers. They married in 1940 and had two daughters, Tricia and Julie. Even Pat didn't realize how big Richard's ambitions were. In 1948, he ran for Congress on the Republican ticket and won a seat in the House of Representatives. But Richard Nixon really wanted to be a senator. In 1950, he ran for Senate. His opponent was a popular Democrat, Helen Gahagan Douglas. Richard Nixon sent out misleading campaign literature, printed on pink paper, suggesting that Douglas was a communist, which was a very bad thing to be in 1950. That's when he got the nickname "Tricky Dick."

Nixon (to speechwriter William Safire, talking about his life in politics): People reach to fear, not love. They don't teach that in Sunday school, but it's true.

FLY ON THE WALL: "Tricky Dick" stuck, and Nixon made quite a name for himself in the Senate, fighting communists with Senator Joe McCarthy, a fellow Republican. So, when Dwight D. Eisenhower was running for president in 1952, he chose Nixon as his running mate. Right after he was nominated, Nixon suddenly became embroiled in a scandal over whether he had used campaign contributions to make himself rich. Eisenhower was about to take him off the ticket, but Nixon went on TV and explained what an honest American he was, in a speech that has become known as the Checkers speech.

People loved the speech. Because of its success, Nixon was kept on the ticket, became vice president in 1952, and was reelected with Eisenhower in 1956. Then in 1960, it was Nixon's turn to run for the presidency.

I should say this—that Pat doesn't have a mink coat, but she does have a respectable Republican cloth coat.

One other thing I probably should tell you, because if I don't they will probably be saying this about me, too. We did get something [from political donors], a gift. . . . It was a little cocker spaniel dog, . . . black and white, spotted, and our little girl Tricia, the six-year-old, named it Checkers. And you know, the kids, like all kids, loved the dog, and I just want to say this, right now, that regardless of what they say about it, we are going to keep it.

Theodore White, historian: No man except Franklin D. Roosevelt campaigned more often for national office across the country than Richard Nixon, who campaigned to be either president or vice president five times.

FLY ON THE WALL: Nixon lost the 1960 campaign, and John F. Kennedy won. But just like in college—in fact, ever since he was a little boy—Nixon's way of bouncing back was to try harder. Right after losing to JFK, he ran for governor of California in 1962. Nixon lost again. This time, he let his anger and hurt show. He famously said to the press, "You won't have Nixon to kick around anymore." But it wasn't true. In 1968, he ran for president again, this time against Democrat Hubert Humphrey. Nixon won—but barely. He was elected president by one of the slimmest margins ever. Four years later, when it came time to run for reelection, he wasn't going to let anything stand in his way.

Nixon: I told my staff that we should come up with imaginative "dirty tricks." The kind that our Democratic opponents used against us.

FLY ON THE WALL: G. Gordon Liddy, the retired FBI agent who became one of the plumbers, saw the 1972 presidential campaign in a larger context.

Liddy: [That] . . . the coming election year would be like no other was apparent. The riots and violence of the past summer, with its attempts to shut down the government of the United States, . . . made it clear that we weren't in for a campaign in 1972. It would be a war.

STRUGGLE AT HOME AND WAR IN VIETNAM

It is difficult now to describe the degree to which the Vietnam struggle defined the late 1960s and early 1970s—in large part because as many as half a million Americans were in uniform in Southeast Asia at any given moment.

—Senator George McGovern, Nixon's opponent in 1972

FLY ON THE WALL: In 1972, the only thing standing between Richard Nixon and four more years of the presidency was the war in Vietnam, which had been going on since 1955. Nixon had campaigned for the presidency in 1968 on a promise that he would "bring an honorable end to the war." Yet even during his campaign, he secretly told members of the South Vietnamese government to hold out and not sign a peace treaty until after the election; he said he would get them a better deal later. Then, once elected, Nixon did *not* end the Vietnam War. In fact, he secretly expanded America's involvement; one-third of the combat deaths in that conflict occurred during his first term in office.

In the late 1960s, as word of the escalation and of war atrocities spread, hundreds of thousands of young people closed down universities, protesting a war they didn't believe in. The world heavyweight boxing champion, Muhammad Ali, registered his protest against the Vietnam War by refusing to be drafted into the army in 1966.

Why should they ask me to put on a uniform and go 10,000 miles from home and drop bombs and bullets on brown people in Vietnam while so-called Negro people in Louisville are treated like dogs and denied simple human rights?

FLY ON THE WALL: Ali, who was stripped of his championship title and sentenced to five years in jail for his antiwar action (though his conviction was later overturned by the Supreme Court), said publicly what many people were saying at home and in the streets. The protest movement kept growing. It was colorful, young, and very noisy. The year that Nixon first became president was the same year that Martin Luther King Jr. and Robert Kennedy were both killed. Their deaths devastated millions of Americans, while others believed that King and Kennedy had been dangerous and radical and had threatened fundamental American values.

Nixon understood that second group. These were the people he had grown up with, the ones he'd lectured on voting when he was only seven. In a speech he gave on November 3, 1969, he named his supporters "the silent majority." He promised that he was listening to them.

> **Eddie Cush, Nixon supporter:** I work my ass off, but I can't make it. I come home at the end of the week, . . . start paying the bills, . . . give my wife some money for food, and there's nothing left. And I pick up the paper, and I read about a million people on welfare in New York . . . or rioting in some colleges. . . . You know [when] you see that you want to go out and strangle someone.

FLY ON THE WALL: Despite the feelings of people like Cush, not all Americans believed in Nixon's vision of America. Nor did all Americans believe that the nation's soldiers should be fighting in Vietnam. Yet Nixon knew that his silent majority hated the antiwar protesters and believed they were unpatriotic, if not downright treasonous.

Nixon (in his acceptance speech at the Republican National Convention, August 8, 1968): We see Americans hating each other; fighting each other; killing each other at home. Did we come all this way for this? Listen to the answer. . . . It is another voice. . . . It is the voice of the great majority of Americans, the forgotten Americans—the non-shouters, the non-demonstrators. This, I say to you tonight, is the real voice of America.

FLY ON THE WALL: While appealing in public to "real" Americans, Nixon privately vowed to continue the military involvement in Vietnam.

Nixon (to his staff): I am not going to be the first American President to lose a war.

FLY ON THE WALL: But other presidents had said the same thing, and neither they nor Nixon chose to tell the truth—which was that the South Vietnamese, backed by the Americans, were losing. In June 1971, the *New York Times* and then the *Washington Post* published an exposé of the way the government had lied to the American people about Vietnam—dating all the way back to the 1950s. The story rested on seven thousand pages of top secret documents that became known as the Pentagon Papers. Even though the Pentagon Papers covered the period before Nixon was elected, he was furious.

Nixon: This is treasonable action on the part of the bastards that put it out. My view is to prosecute the god-damn pricks that gave it to them.

FLY ON THE WALL: The "bastards" turned out to be a military analyst named Daniel Ellsberg who had been in Vietnam. Ellsberg felt the American people had a right to know that their young soldiers were being sent to die in a war that their leaders knew they couldn't win. Ellsberg eventually turned himself in to the authorities and later spoke publicly about his decision to leak the Pentagon Papers to the press.

Ellsberg: This has been for me an act of hope and trust. . . . [I] hope that the truth will free us of this war.

Reporter: Do you have any concern about the possibility of going to prison for this?

Wouldn't you go to prison to help end this war?

FLY ON THE WALL: Ellsberg faced 122 years in jail. The FBI was in charge of the investigation, but Nixon didn't trust the FBI. He wanted his own guys—yup—the plumbers. G. Gordon Liddy, E. Howard Hunt, and Bernard Barker (three of the team who later broke into the DNC headquarters at the Watergate) flew out to California to break into Ellsberg's psychiatrist's office, looking for dirt. They disguised themselves in wigs and hid in the shrubs. Liddy, as usual, acted as mastermind.

> **Liddy:** What did [you] find?

> **Barker:** Nothing, but we ransacked the office, strewing pills on the floor to make it look like junkies looting physicians' offices in search of drugs.

FLY ON THE WALL: Of course, the psychiatrist office break-in was illegal—and they were doing it, as Jeb Magruder noted, because the president's men had ordered them to do it.

> ***North Adams Transcript*, June 16, 1973:** [Magruder testified that] he began to think that if dissenters could break the law, the President's defenders could properly reply in kind.

FLY ON THE WALL: Ellsberg prepared for his trial. The Vietnam War went on. Nixon ordered even more intense bombing of North Vietnam and also of the neighboring countries Cambodia and Laos.

Nixon: The bastards have never been bombed like they're going to be bombed this time.

FLY ON THE WALL: Nixon tried to keep the bombing secret, but people tend to notice bombs falling on their heads. Not only in the United States but also around the world, the demonstrations against the war increased in size and noise. After a particularly violent series of demonstrations in the United States against what people were now calling Nixon's War, Nixon made a television appearance on November 3, 1969.

> **Nixon:** Tonight, I want to talk to you on a subject of deep concern . . . : the war in Vietnam. . . . Honest and patriotic Americans have reached different conclusions as to how peace should be achieved. . . . And so tonight—to you, the great silent majority of my fellow Americans—I ask for your support. . . . As President, I hold the responsibility for choosing the best path to that goal and then leading the nation along it. . . . Thank you and goodnight.

FLY ON THE WALL: The path to peace was much more difficult than Nixon predicted. By 1972, it seemed like the Vietnam War would go on forever. Compared to that, the decision to send a few men to the hotel in the Watergate complex must have, in Nixon's mind, seemed trivial.

PART TWO
THE COVER-UP

WE WON'T LEAVE
ANY PRINTS.

—FRED FIELDING

BLACKMAIL

The only way to get rid of the bills was to shred them.

—G. Gordon Liddy

FLY ON THE WALL: Getting rid of cash isn't usually a problem, but the Watergate plumbers had so much money they worried it would make people suspicious. The day after the break-in, G. Gordon Liddy opened his safe.

> **Liddy:** Sure enough, there were thirteen brand-new hundred-dollar bills . . . cash from the Gemstone treasury. The only way to get rid of the bills was to shred them.

FLY ON THE WALL: Politics and money often go together,

and before 1972 it was perfectly legal to give as much money to politicians as you wanted, and nobody had to know. You could give it in untraceable cash. The advantage of giving a lot of money to a candidate is that you're likely to have an elected official who pretty much has to do what you ask. There is no other name for this except corruption. To keep things about Watergate quiet, money was literally flying around the country. E. Howard Hunt, who was hiding in California, called Liddy a few days after the burglary.

Hunt: Bring money and the name of a lawyer.

Liddy: I arrived at Dulles Airport. I had $5,000 wrapped around each leg, and held in place by elasticized calf-length socks. If my bag was inspected . . . it wouldn't do for the President's Finance Counsel [Liddy's official title] to be flying out of Washington only five days after Watergate.

FLY ON THE WALL: Presidents have a lot of lawyers. John Dean, one of Nixon's lawyers, was hired when he was thirty-one and had practiced law for only six months. That is not enough time to become an expert. But when the White House needed someone to handle Watergate, they chose Dean. Known around the White House as the resident hippie because his hair was at least a quarter inch longer than anybody else's, he was young and eager, dedicated and hardworking. They had plenty for him to do. And they figured that client-lawyer privilege might come in handy.

Jeb Magruder: I called Dean, who had just returned from a trip to the Far East, and asked him to talk to Liddy.

FLY ON THE WALL: Dean agreed, but he got nervous when Liddy appeared in his office in the White House. He already knew that Liddy was the man behind the Watergate break-in.

Liddy: It was obvious that Dean didn't want to be seen with me if he could avoid it. Dean was dressed nattily, his overly long lightened hair flowing over his ears and down beyond his suit coat collar.

FLY ON THE WALL: During the meeting, Liddy tried to put Dean at ease.

Dean: Gordon, I think we ought to take a little walk. . . .

Liddy: Don't worry about it. . . . My men won't talk. But I think it's imperative we get them bailed out. And they expect it. They were promised that kind of support.

Dean: What kind of support?

Liddy: The usual in this line of work. Bail, attorney's fees, families taken care of, and so forth.

FLY ON THE WALL: This was blackmail—the Watergate burglars were really saying, "Give us money, or we'll talk."

Dean: I see. Gordon, I think I'd better be heading back to my office now, and, ah, I really think this is the last conversation we'll ever have. . . .

Liddy: I understand that perfectly. I want you to know one thing. . . . I'm prepared to accept responsibility . . . and if somebody wants to shoot me on a street corner, I'm prepared to have that done. You just let me know where and when, and I'll be there.

Dean: Well, . . . ah, Gordon, . . . I don't think we're really there.

FLY ON THE WALL: Dean had dreamed of being a big shot. Now he was on a park bench, sitting next to a guy who was offering to have himself shot. That was not what John Dean imagined being a White House lawyer would be like.

Then it got worse.

It turned out that Hunt had a safe in the White House, and the White House needed to know what was inside before the FBI came and seized it. The president and his men didn't want to look inside it themselves, in case they might be forced to testify about what was in it. So they made Dean do it.

Dean: Three workmen in green [General Services Administration] overalls and matching green caps wheeled dollies straight into my office and began unloading cartons on my floor. The contents of the safe.

FLY ON THE WALL: Dean and Fred Fielding, a staff member, began to go through the boxes.

Fielding: John, this stuff is sensitive. It could be evidence. Don't you think we ought to be more careful?

FLY ON THE WALL: Fielding was also a lawyer. He remembered that destroying evidence was not what lawyers were supposed to do. He left the office and then returned with two pairs of rubber gloves.

Fielding: Put these on. We won't leave any prints.

FLY ON THE WALL: When Dean and Fielding got a glimpse of the contents of the safe, they were startled, to say the least.

Dean: We found a revolver, which I pinched between two gloved fingers and lifted carefully, as if holding a dead mouse by the tail. . . . Next I lifted out a stack of documents nearly a foot high. [There were] phony State Department cables and a bag full of wiretapping equipment.

FLY ON THE WALL: Dean went to his boss, John Ehrlichman.

Dean: Ehrlichman suggested I "deep-six" the sensitive materials from Hunt's safe by throwing them into the Potomac River.

FLY ON THE WALL: Dean knew that getting rid of evidence was the kind of thing that could definitely land a lawyer in jail. He decided to give the materials in the safe to the acting director of the FBI, L. Patrick Gray, who was a loyal Nixon man.

Dean: These should never see the light of day. They are such political dynamite their existence can't even be acknowledged. I need to be able to say that I gave all Hunt's files to the FBI. That's what I'm doing.

FLY ON THE WALL: Gray knew what Dean wanted him to do. He built a bonfire in his backyard and burned the files—a criminal act.

Gray (just before his death in 2005): I made the gravest mistake of my 88 years in making that decision [to work for Nixon]. . . . This man had not only junked his own presidency but junked the career of so many other people, many of whom had to go to jail.

FLY ON THE WALL: Jail was where James McCord and the other burglars arrested at the Watergate still were.

McCord: It was an overcrowded 100-year-old prison, dank and reminiscent of the European dungeons of a century ago.

FLY ON THE WALL: Burglars who are left to languish in jail get cranky, especially when they know they were hired by some of the most powerful people in the world. Liddy had offered to have himself killed, but as long as he was alive he wanted lots and lots of cash: some for him, and some for his men.

Nixon's staff might not have liked to use the word "blackmail," but they knew it when they saw it. The unusual amount of cash flowing into Nixon's campaign might have raised suspicion if anybody had known about it, but no one outside of Nixon's closest circle had any idea. And just to be clear, we are talking about suitcases stuffed with money, bags of bills, envelopes of cash splitting at the seams.

One of Nixon's lawyers, Herb Kalmbach, was given the job of getting the money to the defendants—in other words, paying them off.

Kalmbach (calling Dean from a phone booth): Meet me in Lafayette Park.

Dean (recalling the meeting): We met soon thereafter in the park and ambled casually to an unoccupied bench.

Kalmbach: It's done.

Dean: We stared off at the feeding pigeons, and he reached down to pat his briefcase softly.

Kalmbach: I've got it right here.

Dean: I was distressed at the thought of being so near the actual cash, and quickly adjourned the meeting.

FLY ON THE WALL: Dean had no intention of being the one left holding the bag—or the money. So he left the briefcase with Kalmbach. But Kalmbach didn't want to be responsible for the money either. He put it in a closet. He didn't know how to give bribes to burglars, their lawyers, or their wives. He needed a "bag man," that is, someone to collect the money and, more important, to drop it off. Luckily for him, there was one handy: Anthony Ulasewicz, known as "Tony U.," a former New York City police officer who did odd—very odd—jobs for the Nixon administration.

Ulasewicz: On June 28, I received a phone call from Herb Kalmbach. . . . A man named Hunt and his wife were exerting a lot of pressure to come up with enough money to cover the bail, attorney's fees, and living fees.

Kalmbach: Dean thinks you're the man to deliver the money. Please take it. I can't tell you what to do with it yet because I don't even know.

Ulasewicz: If you're asking my advice, Herb, when you get into dealing with money this size, sooner or later, word of it leaks out, and more people want a piece of the action. And when money gets involved, big money, so does the possibility of blackmail. Unusual things happen when you start talking about money.

FLY ON THE WALL: Nixon's men were beginning to learn that for themselves.

> **Ulasewicz:** I left the hotel room of the attorney for the President with $75,100 in cash stuffed in a laundry bag tucked under my arm.

FLY ON THE WALL: Ulasewicz had counted the money himself. It turns out that Nixon and his men had counted wrong and missed one of the crisp one-hundred-dollar bills. Delivering money is not as easy as you'd think—some lawyers don't like to be paid with brown paper bags of cash.

> **Ulasewicz:** Running around with $75,100 and trying to get rid of it was a problem.

FLY ON THE WALL: Ulasewicz left packages of cash in airport lockers. Sometimes he hid a package in a phone booth, and once on a window ledge. He had to stay and watch to make sure the right person picked it up. He was good at this job, which was fortunate, because by this point there were a lot of people asking for cash.

UNDER THE BUS: PART I

We would leak out the fact that [Martha's]
not well. . . . Incidentally, [John] can still
do some inside jobs. . . . Then you can use [him]
for the kind of things he is indispensable for.
—Richard Nixon

FLY ON THE WALL: For some journalists, such as Carl Bernstein of the *Washington Post*, Watergate was too juicy a story to go away.

Bernstein: As soon as they called it a third-rate burglary, you knew something was up. There was nothing third-rate about it.

FLY ON THE WALL: Richard Nixon was worried. There were too many places where things could go wrong, too much money flying around the country. He needed somebody to feed to the hungry reporters, somebody higher up than G. Gordon Liddy—a sacrificial lamb. Even though Attorney General John Mitchell was the man Nixon trusted the most, Nixon was not a trusting soul. In the days after the Watergate break-in, Nixon was worried about the sanity of Mitchell's wife, Martha. Martha's habit of calling reporters worried everyone involved with Watergate. A few days after the break-in, Martha Mitchell was out in California for a fund-raiser, alone in a hotel room. Bored, she called Helen Thomas, one of her favorite reporters, to say that she had given her husband an ultimatum: Get out of politics.

Martha Mitchell (confidentially): I'm sick and tired of the whole operation.

FLY ON THE WALL: At that point, Thomas later said, it seemed to her as if someone took the phone out of Martha's hand. Three days later, Martha called Thomas back. This time she finished the conversation, and her words made the front pages.

Martha Mitchell: I am a political prisoner. . . . [They've left me] black and blue. . . . It's horrible to me. . . . I love my husband very much. But I'm not going to stand for all those dirty things that go on. They just don't want me to talk.

FLY ON THE WALL: Once Martha's story made the news, Nixon talked the matter over with his chief of staff, Bob Haldeman.

> Maybe we should send her abroad. You know, Mexico.

> Locking [her] up is a problem.

Nixon: This woman, if she goes completely off her rocker, I don't need that business. She was different before. She wasn't a national celebrity, but now she's a national celebrity. . . .

Haldeman: She started drinking Kahlúa, putting her hand through a window in the hotel, cut her hand all up. They did call a doctor, and stick a needle in her ass, because they had to, she was demolishing the hotel.

Nixon: Incidentally, is she aware of Watergate?

FLY ON THE WALL: Knowing he had to do something quickly, the president invited John Mitchell to lunch. Mitchell and Haldeman had crab soufflé, while the president had his usual pineapple and cottage cheese. They discussed the Martha situation, and again we have that conversation on tape.

> **Nixon (delicately):** Being the wife of a politician is probably infinitely more difficult than being one.

> **John Mitchell:** I think you're right. . . . She gets a little upset about politics, but she loves me, and I love her, and that's what counts.

> **Nixon (continuing carefully):** And Martha's been a great asset to us. I mean, she's a star, she has star quality, she always will, but . . .

FLY ON THE WALL: At the end of the entire Watergate affair, after Nixon had resigned and John Mitchell had gone to jail, Nixon blamed the whole thing on Martha Mitchell.

Nixon: If it hadn't been for Martha, there'd have been no Watergate. Because John wasn't minding that store. He was letting [Jeb] Magruder and these boys, these kids, these nuts run this thing. The point of the matter is that if John had been watching the store, Watergate would never have happened.

FLY ON THE WALL: Barely a week after the Watergate break-in, Nixon and his top aides had come to a conclusion: John Mitchell would have to go.

Nixon: We would leak out the fact that [Martha's] not well. . . . Incidentally, [John] can still do some inside jobs. . . .

Haldeman: It's a beautiful opportunity. He'll gain great sympathy. The Martha fans will think, "Isn't that a wonderful thing." . . . The poor woman hasn't been well and all, and he's going to be by her side and all of that.

FLY ON THE WALL: John Mitchell wrote a moving letter of resignation.

John Mitchell (writing to Nixon): Your words of friendship and understanding when we met today meant more to me than I can possibly convey in this letter. . . .

The moment has come that I must devote more time to the [happiness and welfare of my wife and daughter]. . . .

FLY ON THE WALL: Now the president and his men felt that they could get on with what they thought was the most important business of the summer of 1972: Nixon's reelection.

FOUR MORE YEARS!

After so many rebuffs and disappointments of his career, Richard Nixon was at the zenith of his power. Now it would be full speed ahead.

—Maureen (Mo) Dean, wife of John Dean

FLY ON THE WALL: The 1972 Democratic presidential campaign was a disaster. Thanks in part to Richard Nixon's dirty tricksters, the Republicans were running against a weak Democratic candidate: Senator George McGovern of South Dakota.

McGovern had become a hero to the antiwar movement by sponsoring a bill to cut off funding for the Vietnam War. But that made him unpopular with the rest of the country, who thought he was unpatriotic. Nixon's chief of staff, Bob Haldeman, knew that having an unpopular opponent was to their favor.

Haldeman: The best way to assure that we could win was to pick our opponent. We were much happier with McGovern than other possible foes.

FLY ON THE WALL: The Democratic National Convention in 1972 was so disorganized that McGovern didn't get to make his acceptance speech until 2:28 A.M. EST, when most voters were already asleep. Nixon watched the whole thing from his home in San Clemente, California.

Nixon (joking to his daughter): McGovern is speaking in prime time in Guam.

FLY ON THE WALL: Then things got even worse for the Democrats. McGovern's running mate was Senator Thomas Eagleton, who turned out to have a history of depression. In 1972, that was the sort of thing you didn't admit—especially if you were a politician.

Haldeman: [Eagleton] had been in the hospital three times for mental illness. We were all flabbergasted by that.

Nixon: Survival is the first law of politics and of life.

FLY ON THE WALL: Surprisingly, Nixon did not react with pleasure in learning about the vice presidential candidate's personal history. After the election was over, he wrote privately to Eagleton's thirteen-year-old son, Terry.

Nixon: Politics is a very hard game. . . . What matters is not that your father fought a terribly difficult battle and lost. What matters is that in fighting the battle he won the admiration of foes and friends alike because of the courage, poise, and just plain guts he showed against overwhelming odds.

FLY ON THE WALL: The teenager wrote a sincere reply.

Terry Eagleton (writing from summer camp): Do you know what my dad said when he read your letter: It's going to make it all the tougher to talk against Nixon. I think both Dad and you are excellent politicians. Even though you and Dad don't always agree, I think the country is lucky to have both of you. My favorite subject in school is history. I now feel I am a part of history since you wrote a letter to me.

FLY ON THE WALL: Terry Eagleton *is* a part of history. The letter shows a side of Nixon that the American public rarely saw. His sentimental Checkers speech might have been calculated to have political effect, but he could also feel genuine compassion, even if he usually kept it hidden.

On August 22, 1972, Nixon flew to the Republican National Convention in Miami Beach. He was ready to make a triumphant entrance, but the Secret Service had to clear a path through the noisy antiwar demonstrators who had surrounded the hall shouting slogan after slogan: "Dump Nixon!" "Nixon is a mass murderer!" "Stop the bombing now!" "Two, four, six, eight—organize to smash the state!" "We don't want your [expletive deleted] war!"

Nixon: My eyes burned from the lingering sting of tear gas. As I entered the hall to accept my fifth and last nomination, the delegates shouted . . . "Four more years. Four more years."

FLY ON THE WALL: Nixon, for all his awkwardness, was a masterful politician. Even the original gonzo journalist, Hunter S. Thompson, who wrote for *Rolling Stone* and often made fun of Nixon, noted that Nixon was a tireless campaigner. He admired him for it.

Thompson: He's obviously enjoying this campaign. It's a bonus, a free shot, his last chance to stand eyeball to eyeball again with the high rollers. . . . His instincts are those of a professional gambler who wins more often than he loses.

FLY ON THE WALL: About seventy of every hundred newspapers (71.4 percent) endorsed Nixon in the 1972 election; McGovern received endorsements from only around five of every hundred (5.3 percent). Shortly after the convention, Haldeman handed Nixon the latest Gallup poll. It showed Nixon ahead of McGovern by 34 points, the largest spread in presidential election history.

THE STORY THAT FADES BUT DOESN'T GO AWAY

We had persuaded ourselves that
what we had done, although technically
illegal, was not wrong, or even unusual.

—Jeb Magruder

FLY ON THE WALL: The summer of 1972 was fun for Richard Nixon's men, though not so much for George McGovern's. The Democrats, who knew they were losing, kept hoping that the Watergate scandal would catch fire.

McGovern (speaking in a political campaign ad as headlines about the Watergate break-in flash by): This is about bugging. This is about spying. . . . This is about payoffs. . . . This is about hiding.

This is about dishonesty. . . . This is about hidden funds. . . . This is about the White House.

FLY ON THE WALL: But the public just didn't seem to care.

St. Louis Globe-Democrat, August 17, 1972: Senator George McGovern now appears bent on getting to the White House by tearing down President Nixon with undocumented charges and innuendoes. His latest unsubstantiated smear is a charge that the President is "at least indirectly" responsible for the June 17 break-in at the DNC. . . . He offered no proof of the accusation.

FLY ON THE WALL: But it was a really good story. In the summer of 1972, in the middle of the campaign, two ambitious young journalists from the *Washington Post*, Bob Woodward and Carl Bernstein, homed in on the scandal. Jeb Magruder, focused on Nixon's reelection, was wary of them.

Magruder: We told other reporters the cover story, but we had a policy of never talking to Woodward and Bernstein because they knew too much. There was too great a risk of their asking a question that would trip up one of us.

FLY ON THE WALL: Woodward and Bernstein didn't believe the White House cover story about G. Gordon Liddy going rogue. But they needed proof. All reporters have sources that provide them with information on deep background. In exchange for "inside" information (leaks), the reporter agrees never to reveal the person's name. Among all of their good sources, Woodward and Bernstein had an exceptional one.

Woodward and Bernstein: The managing editor of the *Washington Post* dubbed him "Deep Throat," the title of a celebrated pornographic movie of the time. The name stuck.

FLY ON THE WALL: Deep Throat, it turned out, had an important day job, which is probably why he never met with Woodward and Bernstein in the daylight.

Woodward: We would meet [at] about 2 A.M. on the bottom level of an underground garage.

FLY ON THE WALL: It wasn't until nearly forty years later, in 2005, when Deep Throat was ninety-two years old, that it became publicly known that he was Mark Felt, associate director (second in command) of the FBI. Although Woodward and Bernstein didn't remember Deep Throat ever saying the exact words "Follow the money," which were made famous in the movie *All the President's Men*, he did tell them to try to track down who actually paid the burglars. And, as John Dean noted, they did.

> **Dean:** When [Woodward and Bernstein] uncovered the source of the money used to pay for the break-in, . . . the Re-election Committee's Finance Committee became the target of a long string of stories.

FLY ON THE WALL: As they prepared for the trial of the Watergate burglars, E. Howard Hunt and Liddy had taken the blame, but by now almost nobody believed that they had done it on their own. The big question was, Who hired them? The deputy director of CREEP, Jeb Magruder, had given the actual order for Liddy to go into the Watergate Hotel, so he got ready to play his part in the trial.

> **Magruder:** We had persuaded ourselves that what we had done, although technically illegal, was not wrong, or even unusual. I went to John Dean's office for a dress rehearsal for my session.

FLY ON THE WALL: Dean was coaching Magruder to lie. This is scary stuff. Anyone testifying at a trial has to swear an oath.

Sworn testimony oath in U.S. federal courts:
All the testimony you are about to give in the case now before the court will be the truth, the whole truth, and nothing but the truth; this you do affirm under the pains and penalties of perjury.

FLY ON THE WALL: "Perjury," put simply, is lying under oath. The "pains and penalties of perjury" are prison time. To avoid prison, Magruder needed other people who worked for him to lie, too, especially the ones who had been gathering the money, such as the treasurer of CREEP, Hugh Sloan.

> **Sloan:** I had been ordered to send large chunks of cash from the Treasury to pay for the burglars' expenses.

> **Magruder:** You may have a problem; you may have to find some other way to explain that money. . . .

> **Sloan:** Do you mean commit perjury?

> **Magruder:** You might have to.

FLY ON THE WALL: Hoping to avoid having to lie to the court, Sloan resigned from CREEP that summer. Woodward and Bernstein went to talk to Sloan and his pregnant wife, both of whom seemed terrified.

> **Bernstein (in his and Woodward's 1974 book, *All the President's Men*):** [Sloan] and his wife wanted to get out of Washington. . . . [I] didn't think Sloan would be saying these things unless he was

convinced the White House was involved in the bugging [of the Democratic National Committee] and the cover-up of the true story.

FLY ON THE WALL: Sloan explained to Woodward and Bernstein that the president's men felt themselves to be above the law.

Sloan: People in the White House [believe] they [are] entitled to do things different, to suspend the rules, because they [are] fulfilling a mission—that [is] the only important thing, the mission. It is easy to lose perspective.

FLY ON THE WALL: At this very moment, those men were indeed making up their own rules.

Magruder (during his testimony in court the next summer): [We] began almost by instinct [to] destroy documents, concoct a cover story, and plan perjury.

FLY ON THE WALL: By the end of August, the Watergate story had not gone away. In fact, it was getting bigger. Nixon knew he was going to have to answer more questions about it. Getting John Mitchell to resign hadn't made the story go away. The president's men flew Dean out to California, where Nixon was preparing what he was going to say to the press about Watergate.

Reporter: Mr. President, wouldn't it be a good idea for a special prosecutor to be appointed to investigate the contribution situation and also the Watergate?

Nixon: Under my direction, the counsel to the President, Mr. Dean, has conducted a complete investigation. . . . I can say categorically that his investigation indicates that no one in the White House staff, no one in this Administration, presently employed, was involved in this very bizarre incident.

FLY ON THE WALL: Dean, watching this interview from his hotel room in California, was shocked by it.

Dean: I damn near fell off the bed. . . . I turned off the television. . . . The fact that I had never heard of a "Dean investigation," much less conducted one, did not seem important then.

FLY ON THE WALL: Dean was distracted by how important he suddenly seemed to be.

Dean: I was basking in the glory of being publicly perceived as the man the President had turned to with a nasty problem like Watergate.

FLY ON THE WALL: His wife, Maureen ("Mo"), had a different reaction.

Mo Dean: I knew something the public didn't know: that was that John Dean was very surprised when the

President told a press conference about the Dean investigation. He was surprised because there was no Dean investigation. This disturbed me slightly, but really not very much, because like most Americans, I was convinced there was no White House involvement.

FLY ON THE WALL: Mo Dean was very wrong.

Magruder: There was never any consideration that [we] should tell the truth.

FLY ON THE WALL: Meanwhile, Woodward and Bernstein were getting closer and closer to finding the money they had been following. They had finally connected Mitchell to the payments given to the Watergate burglars.

Bernstein and Woodward (in the *Washington Post*, September 29, 1972): John Mitchell, while serving as U.S. Attorney General, personally controlled a secret Republican fund that was used to gather information about the Democrats, according to sources involved in the White House investigation.

FLY ON THE WALL: The night before the story ran, Bernstein called Mitchell at his home for comment on the article. Mitchell's strong reaction included a threat against the owner of the *Washington Post*, Katharine (Katie) Graham.

Bernstein: Sir, I am sorry to bother you at this hour, but we are running a story in tomorrow's paper that in effect says that you controlled secret funds at the committee while you were Attorney General.

Mitchell: JEEEEESUS, what does it say?

I'll read you the first few paragraphs.

Katie Graham's gonna get her t*# caught in a big fat wringer if that's published. . . . That's the most sickening thing I've ever heard.

FLY ON THE WALL: Back at the *Washington Post*, the reporters and their boss, executive editor Ben Bradlee, realized that Mitchell intended to put pressure on the newspaper, but they had no intention of backing down. Their debate centered on whether they could print the graphic language.

Bradlee: Did Mitchell definitely understand he was talking to a reporter?

Bernstein: Definitely.

Bradlee: Leave everything in but "her t*#" and tell the desk I said it was okay.

FLY ON THE WALL: Woodward and Bernstein printed Mitchell's words as "Katie Graham's gonna get . . . caught in a big fat wringer," but the original statement eventually became public and is now yet another of the famous phrases from Watergate.

ENEMIES, ENEMIES, EVERYWHERE

Somewhere in the 1972 campaign, I said,
"This fellow is going to get himself impeached."
—Representative Thomas P. "Tip" O'Neill,
Democrat from Massachusetts

FLY ON THE WALL: September 15, 1972, was a red-letter day at the White House. Richard Nixon and his men, including White House counsel John Dean, found out that the federal grand jury that had been convened for the case was going to charge only E. Howard Hunt, G. Gordon Liddy, and the five burglars for the Watergate break-in instead of charging the leaders of CREEP, Jeb Magruder and John Mitchell, who had hired them. They were off the hook.

Magruder: I did something I rarely did in my life. I got roaring drunk.

FLY ON THE WALL: The good news for Nixon and his men just kept getting better: The judge announced that the trial would not occur until after the election.

Charleston *News and Courier*, September 19, 1972: As might be expected, federal grand jury indictments in the Watergate caper won't satisfy George McGovern.

FLY ON THE WALL: Indeed, McGovern was not satisfied.

McGovern: It's whitewash . . . and I call for an impartial investigation conducted by somebody entirely outside the Department of Justice.

FLY ON THE WALL: Almost nobody seemed to be listening to McGovern's calls for an investigation. Everyone in the White House figured they had dodged a bullet. Bob Haldeman called in Dean for a meeting with Nixon. Haldeman and Nixon knew that the tapes were spinning, but Dean did not.

Nixon: Well, you had quite a day today, didn't you?

Dean: Quite a three months. I think that we can say that fifty-four days from now [the day of the election], nothing will come crashing down to our surprise. . . .

Nixon: I wouldn't want to be on the other side right

now. . . . They are asking for it. . . . We have not used [our] power in the first four years, as you know.

Dean: That's right.

FLY ON THE WALL: Actually, the Nixon administration had made considerable use of its power. For example, some people would consider secretly expanding the war in Vietnam a use—if not abuse—of power. But that's not what Nixon meant.

> **Nixon:** We haven't used the Bureau [the FBI], and we haven't used the Justice Department, but things are going to change now. . . .

> **Dean:** That's an exciting prospect.

FLY ON THE WALL: With victory in sight, Nixon was ready to go after his enemies, and he had a list—a list he had been keeping for a long time.

> **Nixon:** This is a war.

> **Dean:** I've been keeping [a] list of those who have been "less than our friends."

> **Nixon:** I want the most comprehensive notes on all those who have tried to do us in.

FLY ON THE WALL: The Enemies List, which Chuck Colson and Dean had been compiling since 1971, was one of Nixon's prized projects.

Nixon (in a conversation in the Oval Office soon after his reelection): Never forget: The press is the enemy. The establishment is the enemy. The professors are the enemy. Professors are the enemy. Write that on a blackboard 100 times and never forget it.

FLY ON THE WALL: Nixon's list included almost every reporter who had ever said anything he didn't like. On the eve of his reelection, Nixon and his men wanted to use the power of the government to punish every last person on that list.

Dean (in a memo to Haldeman's assistant, Lawrence Higby): This memorandum addresses the matter of how we can maximize the fact of our incumbency in dealing with persons known to be active in their opposition to our Administration; stated a bit more bluntly—how we can use the available federal machinery to screw our political enemies.

FLY ON THE WALL: The list was quite extensive. During Nixon's first term, the Internal Revenue Service (IRS) had refused to go after his enemies, claiming that the law didn't allow the agency to do so. The IRS collects everybody's taxes, and it's easy to make a mistake on your arithmetic when you're filling out your tax returns. People get nervous when they know the IRS is checking on them, and Nixon liked his enemies nervous. Nixon's goal was to ruin everyone on his Enemies List.

Nixon: It's like a heavyweight fight. I mean, you have

to keep whacking, whacking and whacking. Scare the sh*t out of them.

FLY ON THE WALL: Actually, one person who ended up being scared was George Steinbrenner, the owner of the New York Yankees, who had donated to both sides to cover all the bases, giving to both Republicans and Democrats. But now he was scared to give to the Democrats. He explained his fear to Thomas P. "Tip" O'Neill, the Democratic leader of the House of Representatives.

> **Steinbrenner:** Geez, Tip, I want to tell you what's going on. When they start doing IRS audits on you, there is no way that they're not going to get something on you if they want to.

> **O'Neill:** It was a shakedown. A plain old-fashioned goddammed shakedown. . . . Well, I kept saying to myself, . . . you never can get away with a thing like this. Not in this country. Somewhere in the 1972 campaign, I said, "This fellow is going to get himself impeached." The strange thing about it is that I never gave much thought to the Watergate break-in when it happened. I thought it was silly and stupid. . . . I was concentrating on the shakedown.

A BIG WIN, BUT NOBODY'S HAPPY

**I am at a loss to explain the melancholy
that settled over me that victorious night.**

—Richard Nixon

FLY ON THE WALL: As the election drew closer, Richard Nixon and others in the White House were feeling quite cheerful. According to the latest polls, only 11 percent of the public believed the president was involved with Watergate. It was clear that Nixon was going to win. He and his family flew home to California, where Nixon went to vote. While he was in the booth, surrounded by the press, he dropped his ballot on the floor. The press loved it, but Ron Ziegler, Nixon's press secretary, didn't want any photos of the mishap.

Ziegler: Stop it! Stop it! No pictures!

FLY ON THE WALL: Back in Washington, D.C., several people, including Jeb Magruder, seemed to notice clouds on the horizon.

Magruder: Election night was anti-climactic. . . . The evening was strangely unexciting for me. We had won a great victory . . . yet part of me felt it was a hollow triumph.

FLY ON THE WALL: Nixon himself, who'd flown back to the capital after voting, sat alone in the Lincoln Sitting Room.

Nixon: I am at a loss to explain the melancholy that settled over me that victorious night.

FLY ON THE WALL: Lawrence Higby, to whom John Dean had sent the Enemies List, noticed the president's mood, too.

Higby: It was sort of grim that evening. We thought he'd be saying "We did it! Great job." People were saying, "What's going on?" It was just weird.

FLY ON THE WALL: Nixon's victory was one of the greatest landslides in U.S. history. He won by nearly twenty million votes. Nixon swept everywhere except Massachusetts and the District of Columbia. George McGovern didn't even win his home state of South Dakota.

Dean: The entire senior staff assembled, droopy-eyed and hung-over, the next morning. . . . We rose to our feet . . . to applaud when the President walked in, looking drawn and haggard.

Nixon: This is a great day. Now Bob is going to talk to you about the specifics.

FLY ON THE WALL: Nixon then left the room, and Bob Haldeman, his chief of staff, took charge.

Haldeman: I stood up and in chilling tones . . . told the dumbstruck staff members that each and every one of them must have his resignation on my desk by nightfall.

FLY ON THE WALL: Nixon had been planning this for a long time. He didn't want anyone in the executive branch who wasn't under his complete control.

Nixon (writing about that moment in his memoir): I see this now as a mistake. I did not take into account the chilling effect this action would have on . . . morale.

PART THREE

THE GREAT UNRAVELING

I'LL SHOW THEM I KNOW HOW TO DIE . . .

—G. GORDON LIDDY

BLACK CLOUDS: WITHOUT A SILVER LINING

I don't think we should sit up here like nincompoops.
The function of a trial court is to search for truth.
—Judge John J. Sirica, speaking about the trial
of the Watergate burglars

FLY ON THE WALL: On December 8, 1972, United Airlines Flight 553 from Chicago to New York crashed. All forty-three people on board were killed. One of them was E. Howard Hunt's wife, Dorothy. She had worked for the CIA herself, code name Writer's Wife, and she was the bag woman for the distribution of cash for the Watergate burglars. Anthony "Tony U." Ulasewicz said he'd been instructed to deal with her.

Ulasewicz: She acted like a gambling casino pit boss, . . .

figuring the odds, making sure her cut was secure. . . . She started calculating everybody's needs. . . . She was talking about $400,000 or maybe $450,000.

FLY ON THE WALL: Howard Hunt trusted his wife to collect the money, and he wanted more—a lot more. He called the man he knew was Richard Nixon's fixer, Chuck Colson.

> **Hunt (in phone call to Colson):** Commitments were made to all of us at the onset [that] have not been kept. . . . There's a great deal of financial expense here that has not been covered.

> **Colson:** Okay, you've told me all that. . . . Don't tell me any more. . . .

> **Hunt:** [We] accepted delays because of the election; I want action for Christ's sake.

FLY ON THE WALL: His need for action doubled after he lost his wife. Dorothy Hunt did not survive the plane crash, but her purse did. It contained ten thousand dollars—in hundred-dollar bills.

The White House was worried about both Hunt and Liddy. They knew too much. The only way to be sure they would keep their mouths shut was to promise that when everything was over, the president would pardon them, which means they would get out of jail free.

> **Nixon:** After what happened to Hunt's wife, I think we have a very good case for showing some clemency. After

all, the man's wife is dead, was killed. He's got one child that has—

Colson: Brain damage from an automobile accident.

Nixon: That's right. . . . We'll build up that son of a bitch like nobody's business. We'll have William Buckley [a conservative political commentator] write a column and say, you know, that he should have clemency.

FLY ON THE WALL: The White House sent John Dean to deliver the promise to Liddy.

Dean: Gordon, I want to assure you, everyone's going to be taken care of . . . everyone.

Liddy: Oh . . .

Dean: Absolutely. First, you'll receive living expenses of thirty thousand per annum. Second, you'll have a pardon within two years. . . . Three, we'll see to it you're sent to Danbury Prison [a federal correctional institution in Connecticut known as a "country club prison"]. And fourth, your legal fees will be paid.

Liddy: That's good to hear. . . . I'll keep quiet no matter what.

Dean: I know that, Gordon, but I'll pass it along.

Liddy: Okay. And tell them to watch. I'll show them I know how to die.

FLY ON THE WALL: Oh dear, the White House did not need Liddy to die. They already had enough drama. The Watergate break-in trial started on January 8, 1973, presided over by Judge John J. Sirica.

The jury is going to want to know: What did these men go into that headquarters for? Was their sole purpose political espionage? Were they paid? Who started this? Who hired them? A lot is going to come out in this case.

FLY ON THE WALL: In other words, Sirica was demanding to know everything that Nixon, Dean, Bob Haldeman, and John Ehrlichman had been working on for so many months to keep covered up.

> ***New York Times*, January 8, 1973:** [Hunt arrived] wearing a gray top-coat, a furlike collar and clenching a pipe in his teeth.

FLY ON THE WALL: Even before the jury could be selected, Hunt declared that he had changed his plea to guilty.

Immediately after that, the four Miami burglars also changed *their* pleas to guilty. That meant that they would never have to explain what they were doing at the Watergate. Sirica pressed the burglar Bernard Barker.

> **Sirica:** I don't think we should sit up here like nincompoops. The function of a trial court is to search for truth. What about these hundred-dollar bills that were floating around like coupons?

> **Barker:** I don't know where they came from, Your Honor. I got the money in a blank envelope.

> **Sirica:** I'm sorry, I don't believe you.

FLY ON THE WALL: But Barker revealed nothing.

> ***Boston Globe*, February 1, 1973:** Furthermore, Defendant Barker had no way of knowing who had sent

him $177,000 in checks in a blank envelope to help finance the conspiracy.

FLY ON THE WALL: Sirica set bail at $100,000 and announced that he would delay sentencing for those who had pleaded guilty.

> **Sirica:** I would frankly hope, not only as a judge but as a citizen of a great country, and one of millions of Americans who are looking for certain answers, I would hope that the Senate committee is granted the power by Congress by a broad enough resolution to try to get to the bottom of what happened in this case.

FLY ON THE WALL: Nixon was furious.

> **Nixon:** Here's the judge saying I did this. His goddamn conduct is shocking. He's trying to prod the Senate into a big investigation.

FUZZY EYEBROWS

I'm just an old country lawyer.

—Senator Sam Ervin,

Democrat from North Carolina

FLY ON THE WALL: Richard Nixon had won his landslide in the 1972 election, but his party, the Republican Party, had not gained power in the Senate. In fact, the Democrats had increased their Senate majority by two seats.

Nixon: Our senators are nothing but a bunch of [expletive deleted]. You never get anything from them. All I can say is [expletive deleted] the Senate. You bring them down [to the White House], give them cookies, and you can't count on them.

FLY ON THE WALL: He didn't feel he had to share his victory with the Republican senators. He had not campaigned for them or raised money for them.

Nixon: We won the election. We should let them come to us.

FLY ON THE WALL: Not surprisingly, the Republicans in the Senate and the House knew exactly what Nixon thought of them—and the feeling was mutual. When the Democrats in the Senate proposed forming a committee to investigate the Watergate scandal, the proposal passed by a vote of 77–0. Not one single Republican senator voted to protect Richard Nixon.

Stated purpose of the Senate Select Committee on Presidential Campaign Activities, established on February 7, 1973: To investigate violations of the election laws by the Nixon campaign, and to determine what new reform legislation is needed to prevent any more.

FLY ON THE WALL: And then, when it seemed like it couldn't get worse, the Senate chose North Carolina senator Sam Ervin to chair the committee—which people soon came to refer to as the Ervin Committee. Ervin, a Democrat, was a dramatic southerner with a true flair for words. He loved the media, and the media loved him. That was important because the Watergate hearings were about to be televised, and Americans would be glued to their sets.

Ervin: I'm just an old country lawyer.

FLY ON THE WALL: That was one of Ervin's favorite lines, but it certainly wasn't true. He hadn't gone to a country law school—he had gone to Harvard. He loved to quote his three favorite pieces of literature from memory: the King James Version, the complete works of Shakespeare, and the U.S. Constitution.

Ervin: The United States Constitution is the finest thing to come out of the mind of man.

FLY ON THE WALL: Ervin had big fuzzy eyebrows that he could move wildly up and down when he wanted to. His down-home charm enchanted America, and his loyalty to the Constitution meant that he would hire the smartest and fairest staff he could.

Ervin: The Watergate investigation is a mighty important assignment. It has to be the most thorough and objective inquiry made by the Senate.

FLY ON THE WALL: Still, when the committee started its work, nobody seemed to care about Watergate except the Democrats. Nixon's approval rating stood at 68 percent. Nevertheless, there were going to be hearings, and they were going to be televised.

Nixon: Watergate is starting to snowball. It needs my personal attention.

FLY ON THE WALL: Nixon began organizing and planning his strategy. First, he rallied his troops and assured them he had their backs.

Nixon: I'm not going to let anybody go to jail. That I promise you.

FLY ON THE WALL: There were two problems with this. First, Nixon was never known to keep his promises, and second, some of his men were already in jail, and they weren't very happy about it.

NAMING NAMES

The jail was 104 years old. I looked upward and saw [hordes] of cockroaches running across the ceiling. From time to time, several would drop off onto my body.

—G. Gordon Liddy

FLY ON THE WALL: Meanwhile, back at the District of Columbia's Asylum and Jail, the president's burglars, awaiting their sentencing, were getting restless. G. Gordon Liddy tried to impress the other prisoners by telling them how he would scorch his hand with a candle—his "ordeal by fire" speech—but nobody was impressed. James McCord, in a cell nearby, was in an especially sour mood.

Liddy: McCord actually believed that the United States government wouldn't lie. I think he even felt betrayed by his beloved CIA.

FLY ON THE WALL: McCord saw himself as a martyr. On March 19, 1973, he sat down and wrote a letter to the judge.

McCord (writing to Judge Sirica): In the interests of justice, and in the interests of restoring faith in the criminal justice system, which faith has been severely damaged in this case, I will state the following to you at this time which I hope may be of help to you in meting out justice in this case: . . . There was political pressure applied to the defendants to plead guilty and remain silent.

FLY ON THE WALL: In other words, someone in the government had threatened the Watergate burglars.

McCord: Perjury occurred during the trial in matters highly material to the very structure, orientation, and impact of the government's case, and to the motivation and intent of the defendants.

FLY ON THE WALL: The burglars had lied to the court.

McCord: Others involved in the Watergate operation were not identified during the trial, when they could have been by those testifying.

FLY ON THE WALL: And they had covered up for people.

McCord: The Watergate operation was not a CIA operation. I know for a fact that it was not.

FLY ON THE WALL: Sirica enjoyed drama as much as anyone. Dressed in his robes, he swept into his courtroom, which was crowded with journalists and others interested in the Watergate burglary case. Everyone stood. Then he read McCord's letter out loud, with as much drama as a judge could muster. Reporters raced for the phones outside the courtroom (since this was before you kept your phone in your pocket). Sirica handed down the harshest sentences he could: E. Howard Hunt got thirty-five years, and Bernard Barker, Virgilio Gonzalez, Eugenio Martínez, and Frank Sturgis each got forty years, but the judge made it clear to them (as he hadn't to Liddy) that he would "review" the sentences if they cooperated.

E. HOWARD HUNT (35 YEARS)

BERNARD BARKER (40 YEARS)

VIRGILIO GONZALEZ (40 YEARS)

EUGENIO MARTÍNEZ (40 YEARS)

FRANK STURGIS (40 YEARS)

Sirica: You must understand that I hold out no promises or hopes of any kind to you . . . but I do say that should you decide to speak freely, I would weigh that factor in appraising the sentence . . . and I mean each one of the five of you.

FLY ON THE WALL: The first person Sam Ervin had hired for his committee had been another Sam—law professor Sam Dash, who became the chief counsel in charge of the Watergate investigation.

> **Dash:** When I returned to my office . . . there was a message on my desk: McCord had called. It had only been an hour since Judge Sirica left the bench.

FLY ON THE WALL: When Dash first met McCord, he was surprised.

> **Dash:** I was impressed with McCord's sincerity and earnestness. . . . I believe that McCord is trying to tell us the truth.

FLY ON THE WALL: McCord named names: Jeb Magruder, John Mitchell, and John Dean. Dash knew that Ervin and his committee would want to talk to those men, and this time it would be under oath.

A CANCER ON THE PRESIDENCY

We could get a million dollars . . . and you could
get it in cash. I know where it could be gotten.
There is no problem in that.

—Richard Nixon

FLY ON THE WALL: Many of Richard Nixon's men were starting to plan their escape routes. John Dean warned his wife, Mo, that the situation was serious.

Mo Dean: He told me things were getting so rough that he might even have to go to prison.

FLY ON THE WALL: But John Dean wanted one chance to lay everything out in front of the president. He still wanted to believe that Nixon hadn't really known everything that was going on.

He showed up at the Oval Office on March 21, 1973. He had never before been alone with the president. Now it was just the two of them—and the tape machine, which Dean didn't know about. Nixon had his feet up on his desk and looked relaxed.

Dean: We have a cancer—within, close to the presidency, that's growing. It's growing daily.

FLY ON THE WALL: Nixon's feet came off his desk. The young lawyer had Nixon's full attention.

Dean: We're being blackmailed.

FLY ON THE WALL: Something like this would be hard to say out loud whether or not you know you're being taped. Of course, it wasn't hard for Nixon to hear, because he was the one who had arranged the first blackmail money, months ago.

People are going to start perjuring themselves very quickly.

FLY ON THE WALL: This got Nixon's attention.

Dean: So let me give you sort of the basic facts.

FLY ON THE WALL: Dean explained just how much it had cost to keep G. Gordon Liddy, E. Howard Hunt, and the other burglars quiet so far.

Nixon: How much money do you need?

Dean: These people are going to cost a million dollars over the next two years.

Nixon: We could get a million dollars . . . and you could get it in cash. I know where it could be gotten. There is no problem in that.

FLY ON THE WALL: The president of the United States had just been caught on tape, discussing the best way to supply endless amounts of cash for blackmail. But a funny thing happened on the way.

Dean: People around here are not pros at this sort of thing. This is the sort of thing Mafia people can do, washing money, getting clean money, things like that. We are not criminals and not used to dealing in that business.

FLY ON THE WALL: In truth, Nixon was interested in only one thing: getting the scandal as far away from himself as he could. He sent Dean up to Camp David, the presidential retreat in Maryland, to write the report he had promised people back in September, six months earlier.

Mo Dean: After he told President Nixon that there was

a cancer on the presidency, John thought the President would try to get at that truth and then bring a quick end to the cover-up; but instead the talk was about writing a report that would "clear" just about everybody. So that's what he was doing at Camp David: trying to write a report that was impossible to write.

FLY ON THE WALL: But Nixon didn't think it was at all impossible. He had already told John Dean what the report was supposed to find. Dean's job was just to keep it far from the truth.

Nixon (to Dean): Don't, don't go into . . . we investigated this, we investigated that. Lay off of all that. . . . Just . . . No one in the White House staff was involved, you see?

FLY ON THE WALL: This was tricky because a lot of the White House staff was already in jail for being involved.

Nixon: It's your view the vulnerables are basically, Mitchell, Colson, and Haldeman . . . right?

Dean: And I'd say Dean to a degree. . . .

Nixon: You . . . Why?

Dean: Well, because I have been all over this thing like a blanket.

FLY ON THE WALL: The truth was devastating to Dean's wife.

Mo: John Dean III, my beloved husband, the President's counsel, a criminal.

UNDER THE BUS: PART II

FLY ON THE WALL: John Dean wasn't a fool. He knew trouble was coming at him from all sides, as his wife, Mo, later noted.

Mo Dean: John had to look after his own flanks . . . because it was clear [that everybody else] was so obviously looking after their own flanks.

FLY ON THE WALL: It was time for John Dean to get his own lawyer, so he hired the experienced Charles Shaffer.

Shaffer: John, you're in big trouble . . . serious trouble.

Dean: I expected my lawyer to be more encouraging.

FLY ON THE WALL: Dean knew that the only way for him to stay out of jail was to make a deal for immunity—which means that Congress would give him a "Get out of jail free" card. His lawyer, Shaffer, set up a meeting with Sam Dash, chief counsel of the Ervin Committee.

> **Dash:** John Dean told me a fantastic story. The most shocking revelation was Dean's account of a meeting he had with the President. . . . This was the first real indication of the President's involvement in the Watergate cover-up. Dean was an essentially unremarkable person; at the time of our meeting, he saw himself as a young lawyer who had pulled himself out of a powerful conspiracy and was expiating the wrongs he had been committing by his willingness to expose them to the public. This is a real break-through.

FLY ON THE WALL: Dean had convinced himself that he was a victim, and he had convinced Dash. Washington being what it was, Richard Nixon found out that Dean was talking to his prosecutors. Nixon called him in for one last meeting on April 16, 1973.

> **Dean:** [Nixon] seemed exhausted, slurring his words and looking remarkably rumpled. He took me through a series of leading questions . . . that made me wonder if he was recording me. . . . He even brought up the cancer on the presidency . . . and said that of course, when he said that he could raise a million dollars, he had been joking.

FLY ON THE WALL: Nixon knew he couldn't trust Dean anymore. And the tapes were whirring. Nixon consulted with Henry Petersen, head of the Criminal Division of the Justice

Department, who told him not only that he had to fire Dean, which Nixon didn't mind, but also that it was time to cut loose his two closest advisers, Bob Haldeman and John Ehrlichman. That one really hurt.

Petersen: Mr. President, what you have to realize is that these two men have not served you well. They already have, and in the future will, cause you embarrassment, and embarrassment to the presidency.

Nixon: I can't fire men simply because of the appearance of guilt. I have to have proof of their guilt.

Petersen: What you have just said, Mr. President, speaks very well of you as a man. It does not speak well of you as a president.

FLY ON THE WALL: But, no, it didn't speak well of anybody. Even so, Nixon had already made up his mind. To save himself, he was going to get rid of his closest aides. He called them to Camp David to explain.

Haldeman: The P [president] was in terrible shape. He shook hands with me, which is the first time he's ever done that.

FLY ON THE WALL: As they walked through the gardens of Camp David, blooming with tulips and lilacs, Nixon told Haldeman he would have to resign and said that he'd been dreading this conversation.

> When I went to bed last night, I hoped and almost prayed that I wouldn't wake up this morning.

FLY ON THE WALL: Haldeman came out of his meeting and met Ehrlichman on his way in.

>**Haldeman:** Your turn.
>
>**Ehrlichman:** How did it go?
>
>**Haldeman:** About as expected.

FLY ON THE WALL: Nixon went through the same speech he had given Haldeman. Ehrlichman later reported that Nixon began crying uncontrollably.

>**Nixon:** It's like cutting off my arms. . . . You and Bob, you'll need money. I have some—and you can have it.
>
>**Ehrlichman:** That would just make things worse. You can do one thing, though, sometime. Just explain

all this to my kids, will you? Tell them why you had to do this.

FLY ON THE WALL: Later, Haldeman was hurt to learn that Nixon had used the exact same words with both of them about praying not to wake up.

Haldeman: I had been moved and felt a kinship with him. Now I see that this was just a conversational ploy—a debater's way of slipping into a difficult subject—used on both of us.

FLY ON THE WALL: On April 30, 1973, Nixon went on national television and, for the first time ever, spoke to the American people about Watergate—in a twenty-four-minute speech in which he claimed that he'd known nothing about the cover-up until he talked to Dean on March 21.

Nixon: There can be no whitewash in the White House.

FLY ON THE WALL: Nixon then announced that Haldeman and Ehrlichman would be leaving his administration.

Nixon: Today, in one of the most difficult decisions of my presidency, I accepted the resignation of two of my closest associates in the White House, Bob Haldeman [and] John Ehrlichman, two of the finest public servants it has been my privilege to know.

FLY ON THE WALL: Ehrlichman and Haldeman got all that praise—Dean got none. The president gave him just ten words.

Nixon: The Counsel to the President, John Dean, has also resigned.

FLY ON THE WALL: When Nixon finished his speech, he got drunk. Feeling very sorry for himself, he called Haldeman, the man he had just fired, for sympathy.

Nixon (to Haldeman): I'm never going to discuss the son-of-a-bitch Watergate thing again—never, never, never, never.

IMPEACHMENT ON THE HORIZON

The Watergate whirlpool is swirling so swiftly
now that it threatens to create an atmosphere
approaching hysteria . . . particularly in Washington
and in segments of the press. Impeachment is not an
impossible turn in this crazy pattern of surprises.
—*Tulsa World*, May 10, 1973

FLY ON THE WALL: After his televised speech, Richard Nixon thought that most of America would clasp him to their hearts the way they had after the Checkers speech, the one about his little dog. Not this time.

St. Louis Post-Dispatch, **May I, 1973:** The resignation of three of Mr. Nixon's closest associates and the firing of ... John Dean III, have confirmed ... that those who have sat at the right hand of Mr. Nixon were implicated or compromised by the crime. Had Watergate occurred in any other Western democracy, the government would have fallen long ago.

FLY ON THE WALL: Nixon was shocked when a Gallup poll right after the speech showed that 50 percent of the population didn't believe him.

> ***Chicago Tribune*, May I, 1973:** The Watergate dam burst yesterday. And four top administration officials were swept out of office in the biggest White House purge in memory.

FLY ON THE WALL: By May 10, his standing in the polls had fallen below 48 percent for the first time since he had become president. Some newspapers, such as or New York's *Amsterdam News*, the oldest black paper in the country, had begun talking about getting rid of Nixon altogether.

> ***Amsterdam News*, May 5, 1973:** These Watergate scoundrels are the very persons responsible for the destructive social policies that ignored the needs of urban America and denied justice, liberty, and opportunity to the poor and the black. Congressman Charles Rangel has called for impeachment of Nixon on the grounds that his official conduct leaves much to be desired.

FLY ON THE WALL: To impeach a U.S. president, the House of Representatives must vote, by a simple majority, to bring formal charges of wrongdoing. Following the impeachment, the Senate places the president on trial; removal from office happens only if two-thirds of the Senate decides that the president is guilty of the charges.

IMPEACHMENT PROCESS

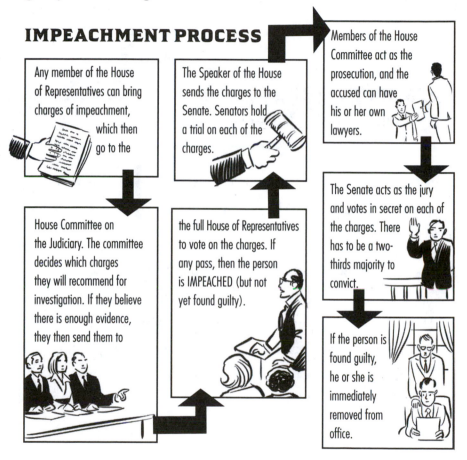

Any member of the House of Representatives can bring charges of impeachment, which then go to the

House Committee on the Judiciary. The committee decides which charges they will recommend for investigation. If they believe there is enough evidence, they then send them to

the full House of Representatives to vote on the charges. If any pass, then the person is IMPEACHED (but not yet found guilty).

The Speaker of the House sends the charges to the Senate. Senators hold a trial on each of the charges.

Members of the House Committee act as the prosecution, and the accused can have his or her own lawyers.

The Senate acts as the jury and votes in secret on each of the charges. There has to be a two-thirds majority to convict.

If the person is found guilty, he or she is immediately removed from office.

***Worcester Telegram*, May 6, 1973:** Speculation about impeachment of President Nixon rests on the possibility that he may be implicated so deeply in the Watergate scandal as to make it clear that he conspired to break the law.

FLY ON THE WALL: At the time of Nixon's presidency, the country hadn't faced the impeachment of a president in more than one hundred years—that of Andrew Johnson in 1868, during the aftermath of the bloody Civil War. So the possibility put people—like the Speaker of the House, Tip O'Neill—on alert.

> **O'Neill:** The time is going to come when impeachment is going to hit this Congress, and we better be ready for it.

FLY ON THE WALL: Of course, not everybody was willing to accept the idea yet that the president was a criminal and should be impeached.

> ***Burlington Free Press*, May 15, 1973:** We are appalled by the sewer of hatred which the anti-Nixon [force] is spewing over this land. The Watergate case is nowhere near as poisonous as is this irrational splash of hatred.

ARCHIBALD COX
TO THE RESCUE

**[Archibald Cox was a] partisan viper . . .
planted in our bosom.**

—Richard Nixon

FLY ON THE WALL: Before the Watergate hearings even began, another much anticipated case was coming to trial—that of Daniel Ellsberg, the man who had released the Pentagon Papers, outlining the government's secret actions in the Vietnam War. The biggest sensation from that trial, however, turned out not to be Ellsberg himself. Instead, the shock came when the Justice Department told the judge that Richard Nixon's plumbers were the ones who had broken into Ellsberg's psychiatrist's office.

Ellsberg: I wish I could say as a citizen that I'm

surprised. How can [we] be surprised just because the administration breaks the law?

FLY ON THE WALL: The press jumped on the story.

Washington _Evening Star_, May 8, 1973: On and on come the ugly revelations, the almost daily disclosure of how this nation's political and judicial processes have been manipulated and corrupted.

FLY ON THE WALL: Public outcry grew. In the United States, when there are controversial issues involving the president, the U.S. attorney general—the head of the Justice Department—appoints a special prosecutor to clean up the mess. Hoping to keep that from happening, Nixon appointed his secretary of defense, Elliot Richardson, as his new attorney general. He figured that Richardson's reputation for integrity would mean that there would be no need for a special prosecutor.

Nixon (speaking to one of his aides about Richardson): He's sort of Mr. Integrity, Mr. Clean . . . because he would be trusted by the so-called damned establishment.

FLY ON THE WALL: During his televised speech on April 30, 1973, Nixon had announced the appointment and outlined Richardson's role.

Nixon: I have given him absolute authority to make all decisions bearing upon the prosecution of the Watergate case and related matters.

FLY ON THE WALL: But in private Nixon had very different instructions for his new attorney general.

> **Nixon:** Elliot, the one thing they're going to be hitting you on is about the special prosecutor.
>
> **Richardson:** Yeah.
>
> **Nixon:** The point is I'm not sure you should have one.
>
> **Richardson:** I'll think about it, sir.

FLY ON THE WALL: The members of the Senate had their own ideas—they refused to confirm Richardson unless they were promised that there would be a special prosecutor. The Senate wouldn't give in, and Richardson, as the new attorney general, was given the sole authority to appoint a special prosecutor. He chose Archibald Cox, who had been one of his professors at Harvard Law School. Journalist J. Anthony Lukas of the *New York Times* wrote:

> **Lukas:** [Cox had] an unmistakable pale patrician air, hair crew-cut, with a predilection for three-piece suits, tweeds, bow ties, nubby sweaters.

FLY ON THE WALL: At Cox's own Senate confirmation hearings, West Virginia senator Robert Byrd asked if he would follow the Watergate trail as far as it would go.

> **Byrd:** Even though that trail should lead, Heaven forbid, to the Oval Office of the White House?

Cox: Wherever that trail may lead . . . my main task is to restore confidence in the honor, integrity, and decency of government.

FLY ON THE WALL: Cox was just the kind of person who had tormented Nixon ever since he was a small boy.

Nixon: If [Elliot Richardson] had searched specifically for the man whom I would have least trusted, he could hardly have done better. [Archibald Cox was a] partisan viper . . . planted in our bosom.

EVERYBODY'S WATCHING

On May 17, 1973, 11 months after the
5 burglars were apprehended at Watergate,
the electronic media took over.

—Gladys Engel Lang and Kurt Lang, *The Battle for Public Opinion*

FLY ON THE WALL: Senator Sam Ervin, the one with the fuzzy eyebrows and charming southern accent, had a colorful wooden gavel that had been handmade by the Cherokee. And on May 17, 1973, he banged it down to open the Watergate hearings.

> **Ervin:** The Founding Fathers knew that those who are entrusted with power are susceptible to the disease of tyrants . . .

. . . breaking into the home of everyday citizens . . . not for the jewels . . . [but] something much more valuable . . . their right to vote in their own elections.

FLY ON THE WALL: All three major television networks—NBC, CBS, and ABC—covered the hearings, as did the noncommercial Public Broadcasting Service (PBS). For four months, Americans could watch the hearings at least part of every day. As noted by communications specialists Gladys Engel Lang and Kurt Lang in *The Battle for Public Opinion*, people were glued to their TVs that summer.

> **Gladys and Kurt Lang:** By the second week of hearings, almost three out of four television homes had tuned in. By early August . . . 90 percent of all Americans had watched some of the hearings.

FLY ON THE WALL: Ervin, the senator who claimed to be "just a country lawyer," was suddenly hailed as the savior of the country. He carried around a little blue pocket edition of the Constitution that he'd shake at witnesses. At first, Richard Nixon thought that Ervin wouldn't be much of a problem.

> **Nixon (talking to his new chief of staff, Alexander Haig , June 13, 1973):** They don't realize what they're up against—this stupid Ervin, drinking too much and pointing his finger. Ha!

FLY ON THE WALL: Ervin's committee hearing room, packed with TV cameras, became the place to be. Outside, bumper stickers read HONK IF YOU THINK HE'S GUILTY!—which led to some really noisy traffic jams. Of course, not everybody was honking. Some thought the Watergate hearings were a "witch hunt," and Nixon was still their man.

> **Terry, a bar owner in Astoria, Queens, New York, on the first day of the hearings:** You need a strong man at the top—to whip people into shape. . . . It might scare some people . . . [but it] doesn't scare me.

FLY ON THE WALL: James McCord testified on television, and it was pretty interesting if you wanted to know how to bug a phone. Anthony "Tony U." Ulasewicz became a big hit, telling Congress how he'd acted as a bag man. Other witnesses mostly said they were sorry, but everybody was waiting for John Dean. Rumors were flying.

Dean: The White House was betting that millions of people did not wish to believe a man who called the President a liar.

FLY ON THE WALL: Dean saw his testimony as a chance to save his reputation, or what was left of it. He and his wife, Mo, prepared carefully.

Mo Dean: Much of the nation sat on the edge of its chair on Sunday, June 24, 1973. John and I slumped in ours.

FLY ON THE WALL: A lawyer told Dean to wear glasses so that he would look more serious. Mo planned her whole week's wardrobe.

Mo Dean: I relied on my own fashion instinct, choosing a very high-collared tan dress to wear on the first day. On Tuesday, I picked out a combination that I loved: a brown linen dress. . . . Wednesday, I wore a floral blouse with a melon-red suit, Thursday, a white blouse with a bright yellow linen suit. . . . On Friday, I wore a burgundy blouse with white polka dots, a white skirt, and a navy-blue blazer.

FLY ON THE WALL: As many as eighty million Americans watched at least part of Dean's testimony. Mo Dean had a seat in the front row, right behind John.

Mo Dean: I was vaguely aware of a blur of faces. Soon a big man with white hair . . . bushy eyebrows and jelly-like jowls took his seat. Occasionally, I became aware

of the photographers
massed in front of us. . . . At the
end of the long day, John's sincerity and truthfulness had
come through . . . not to everyone, but to many.

FLY ON THE WALL: In fact, polls showed that more than half
of those polled didn't believe Dean; they thought he was disloyal
to Nixon and was just out to save his own skin. On the second
day of the hearings, Dean, speaking before Connecticut senator
Lowell Weicker, dropped what seemed like a casual comment.

Dean: I have in my possession a memorandum that was
requested of me—to prepare a means to attack the enemies of the White House. . . . An enemies list.

Weicker: I wonder, are those documents in the possession of the committee?

Dean: No . . . but I would be happy to submit them.

FLY ON THE WALL: Dean wasn't just happy; he was eager. All of a sudden, the burning question was not whether Dean was a liar; instead, everyone wanted to see the list. Daniel Schorr, a CBS reporter, read the list on live TV. Not too far into the list, he came upon a surprise.

> **Schorr (speaking years later about the incident):** "Number 17, Daniel Schorr, a real media enemy." I almost collapsed on the air.

FLY ON THE WALL: Again, the media pounced. Tom Wicker, a writer for the *New York Times* who was also on the list, wrote:

> **Wicker:** I have had a mixed reaction to being named on a long "master list" of enemies of Richard Nixon. . . . The [list confirms] what the 1970 internal security plan and the Ellsberg break-in suggested—that the Watergate burglary itself was only the tip of the knife, that American democracy has been retrieved in the nick of time from the police state it so nearly became.

FLY ON THE WALL: As the Watergate hearings went on, millions watched as John Ehrlichman argued that he and the president hadn't done anything wrong. They had, he claimed, the right to break the law.

> **Ehrlichman (testifying at the Watergate hearings):** The action of the plumbers fits well within the president's inherent constitutional powers.

FLY ON THE WALL: The senators, including Democrat Herman Talmadge of Georgia, didn't see it that way. Breaking and entering was illegal, no matter who was doing it.

> **Talmadge:** There is a famous principle of law that came from England and also is well-known in this country, that no matter how humble a man's cottage is—that even the king of England cannot enter without his consent.

> **Ehrlichman:** I'm afraid that has been considerably eroded over the years.

> **Talmadge:** Down in my country, we still think it is a pretty legitimate principle of law.

FLY ON THE WALL: Were the buggings, the break-ins, and the Enemies List all legal just because they were done in the president's name? The vocal minority of people who had opposed Nixon said no, and they felt that the hearings offered a satisfying proof that they had been right all along. But Nixon's supporters—the silent majority—felt that their world was coming undone. And it was frightening.

> **Kathy Vierra, citizen interviewed about the hearings:** It's unbelievable that something like this should happen in this country, it's supposed to be so great. It makes me feel so unprotected. Things aren't as steady and sound as I thought. They are kind of crumbling apart.

TAPES, TAPES, WHO'S GOT THE TAPES?

Mr. Nixon has tried mightily to portray the approaching confrontation with Senator Ervin's select committee as a kind of constitutional high noon.
—*Washington Post*

FLY ON THE WALL: As the Watergate hearings continued to get high ratings on television, some people became stars. Sam Ervin was a natural. But even Howard Baker, senator from Tennessee, who was not a charismatic man, had his moment of celebrity.

Baker: What did the president know, and when did he know it?

FLY ON THE WALL: In fact, he asked the same question so many times that political comics such as Marty Nadler started using it as a punch line.

> **Nadler:** Did you hear about the new Watergate watch? Both hands always point to Nixon.

FLY ON THE WALL: For Richard Nixon's silent majority, Watergate wasn't funny. It was betrayal.

> **Betty Bennett, citizen:** I wanted to feel that the President didn't know, but I know that's not true. I truly feel that he knew, and it hurts me. It makes me feel terrible.

Alexander Bennett, Betty's husband and a policeman:

Ever since I was a little kid I was taught respect for the President and the country. Now when I arrest a teenager . . . Why are you picking on me? The president is corrupt, and he steals.

FLY ON THE WALL: As the hearings went on, things just got more confusing. Details that nobody expected started slipping out, and each one meant that *somebody* had lied. But who? If John Dean was telling the truth, then the president and the White House were lying. Some people just didn't want to believe that. Some people thought that to even suggest such a thing was treason. It all depended on who was telling the truth. Senator Herman Talmadge kept pressing for answers.

Talmadge: What makes you think that your credibility is greater than that of the President, who denies what you have said?

Dean: Well, Senator, I have been asked to come up here and tell the truth. . . . I'm telling you what I know. I'm telling you just as I know it.

FLY ON THE WALL: During his testimony, Dean let hints fall that maybe—perhaps—the White House had been bugged by Nixon himself. A few weeks after Dean's testimony, the Ervin Committee's chief counsel, Sam Dash, had a private conversation with him.

John, let me ask you this. Do you think it's possible Nixon could have taped all of his office and phone conversations?

. . . Sure, it's possible.

Dash: How could we find out?

Dean: Sam, if he did, I'll tell you who would probably know . . . Alexander Butterfield.

FLY ON THE WALL: On July 16, 1973, the TV networks all got word that there was a mystery witness with bombshell testimony. Excited, all the networks went live as Fred Thompson, the chief minority counsel on the Ervin Committee, began questioning Nixon's deputy assistant.

Thompson: Mr. Butterfield, are you aware of the installation of any listening devices in the Oval Office?

FLY ON THE WALL: Butterfield took a deep breath while everyone in America waited. The pause seemed to go on forever.

Butterfield: I was aware of listening devices, yes, sir.

FLY ON THE WALL: Butterfield went on to talk about the details, but nobody was listening. Nobody could get past the idea that there were secret tapes. Finally, it might be possible to know who was telling the truth.

New York Times, **July 17, 1973:** The tape recordings, which Mr. Butterfield said had been stored in the Executive Office Building by the Secret Service, theoretically could prove or disprove the explosive—but undocumented—charge by Mr. Dean, the former counsel to the President, that Mr. Nixon was deeply involved in the Watergate cover-up.

FLY ON THE WALL: The day that Butterfield testified, Nixon was spitting up blood. He ended up in the hospital with pneumonia. His new top aides, including Vice President Spiro Agnew, came to see him.

> **Agnew:** Boss, you've got to have a bonfire.

FLY ON THE WALL: But who should light the match? The best idea was Nixon's dog, King Timahoe, a springer spaniel. They were kidding about the dog, but not entirely about the bonfire. The tapes were still in Nixon's possession, and no one yet had ordered him to give them up. Nixon decided he wasn't going to destroy the tapes. He still had visions of writing his own history—which would remember him as a great president. He would keep the tapes, and he wouldn't let anyone else listen to them either. Instead he would claim executive privilege. Executive privilege is the idea that the president's writings and conversations are special and private: That's the privilege part. Nixon was claiming that because he was president, not only were *his* words private, but so was everything that anybody else ever said *to* him. Therefore, nobody who spoke to the president ever had to testify about what he or she said—even if it was about being ordered to do break-ins.

> **Nixon:** If the president broke the confidence of those who unburdened themselves in his office, it would shatter the presidency.

FLY ON THE WALL: Nixon seemed to believe that. But neither

Congress nor the Ervin Committee nor Archibald Cox agreed. They wanted those tapes.

> **Ervin:** No writ of executive privilege extends to either alleged illegal activities or political activities.

FLY ON THE WALL: Nixon was saying that the man and his job were separate things, that whoever was in the president's office didn't have to obey any court orders or tell the truth under oath. He believed it to his dying day.

> **Nixon:** Well, when the president does it, that means that it is not illegal.

FLY ON THE WALL: That phrase has remained one of the most famous Watergate quotes, decorating mugs and other souvenirs available at the Nixon Library gift shop. But the idea that the president, or any other officeholder, is above the law violates the whole idea of American government. The stage was set for a battle.

THE LAW VERSUS RICHARD NIXON

If we have a confrontation, we will have it.
If Cox does not agree, we will get rid of Cox.
—Alexander Haig, Nixon's chief of staff,
to Elliot Richardson, attorney general

FLY ON THE WALL: Richard Nixon wrote a polite, firm letter to Archibald Cox, the special prosecutor, explaining that, in order to protect the presidency, he could not turn over the tapes. Bright and early the next day, Cox showed up in Judge John J. Sirica's office, requesting a subpoena, which is a court order demanding that you have to do something, whether you want to or not, and if you don't do it, you go to jail.

In Re: Subpoena to Nixon: Order that respondent,

President Richard M. Nixon, or any subordinate officer, . . . is hereby commanded to produce forthwith . . . the subpoenaed documents or objects [i.e., the tapes].

FLY ON THE WALL: Nixon dug in his heels.

Nixon: With the utmost respect for the court . . . the President is not subject to compulsory process from the courts.

FLY ON THE WALL: Journalists understood now that the Watergate hearings were about far more than a small-scale break-in.

Newsday: The impending clash threatens political and constitutional fallout far more destructive than the Watergate scandal itself.

FLY ON THE WALL: But did Nixon understand?

Nixon: I will not tear down the office of the American presidency for Watergate.

FLY ON THE WALL: The world seemed to be unraveling.

Mary Conners, citizen: I have a four-year-old who watches the hearings and keeps asking if they are going to put the President in jail.

FLY ON THE WALL: Still, Nixon had plenty of loyal supporters. His poll numbers showed that his silent majority still stood with him.

James Conners, citizen and Westchester, New York, lawyer: The hearings are very political, and I think the Chairman, Sam Ervin, is very anti-Nixon. I don't think the criticisms against him have much basis in fact.

Noel Looney, citizen: There are probably things we shouldn't know about. Maybe some things are beyond our capacity to understand.

FLY ON THE WALL: There were plenty of people on Nixon's staff, such as his speechwriter Patrick Buchanan, who still believed that Nixon could convince the public he was keeping the tapes from them for their own good. J. Anthony Lukas quotes Buchanan in his groundbreaking book *Nightmare: The Underside of the Nixon Years.*

Buchanan: Our adversaries . . . wish to castrate the President . . . to reverse the democratic verdict at the polls. . . . They fully intend the exploitation of this scandal to cancel the Nixon counter-revolution. If we have to drift into demagoguery so be it—we owe them a few.

FLY ON THE WALL: Demagogues are leaders who appeal to people's fear and prejudices. They gain their power by exploiting the worst in people: They encourage them to blame their problems on a group of "others" and promise them that by destroying that group, everyone else will be fine. In a televised speech on August 15, 1973, Nixon seemed to blame the Watergate break-in on hippies.

JOSEPH McCARTHY
SENATOR, U.S.
1947–1957

ADOLF HITLER
CHANCELLOR, GERMANY
1933–1945

BENITO MUSSOLINI
PREMIER, ITALY
1922–1943

GAIUS FLAMINIUS
POLITICIAN, ROMAN EMPIRE
232–217 B.C.E.

CLEON
GENERAL, ATHENS
C. 431–422 B.C.E.

Nixon: In the 1960s . . . individuals and groups increasingly asserted the right to take the law into their own hands, insisting that their purposes represented a higher morality. . . . That same attitude brought a rising spiral of violence and fear, of riots and arson and bombings, all in the name of peace and in the name of justice. . . . It is not surprising, even though it is deplorable, that some persons, in 1972, adopted the morality that they themselves had rightly condemned and committed acts that have no place in our national system.

FLY ON THE WALL: The speech didn't sit well with many people, including Republican senator Edward Brooke of Massachusetts.

Brooke: The people want the facts. The President gave us rhetoric.

FLY ON THE WALL: Nixon was an expert at appealing to people's fears and prejudices, but this time it didn't work. Nixon's refusal to give up the tapes was turning the public against him. More than half of the public—54 percent—believed that Congress would be justified in beginning impeachment proceedings if Nixon resisted the court order to turn over the tapes. Only 24 percent thought he shouldn't be impeached. The rest of the public wasn't sure.

Nixon: Why doesn't the President resign because his popularity is low? Because if the time comes . . . when the President makes decisions based on where he stands in the polls, rather than what is right or wrong, we have a very weak President.

FLY ON THE WALL: Rumors started spreading around the country, and many of them were cruel.

Nixon: At some point in the hot muggy summer of 1973, some of the most influential members of the Washington press corps concluded that I was starting to go off my rocker.

FLY ON THE WALL: In September, as the courts were deciding whether or not Nixon would have to surrender the tapes, the news broke that Nixon's vice president, Spiro Agnew, had been taking bribes from practically everybody in his home state of Maryland and, on top of that, not paying his taxes. Agnew resigned on October 10, 1973. Although his criminal actions had nothing to do with Watergate, his resignation added to the feeling that things were falling apart. To replace Agnew, Nixon appointed Gerald Ford, a Republican congressman from Michigan and one of the few members of the House who was respected by both Democrats and Republicans—respected, that is, by everyone except Nixon.

> **Nixon (sarcastically, sitting behind his desk in the Oval Office):** Can you imagine Gerry Ford in this chair?

FLY ON THE WALL: On October 12, 1973, two days after Agnew's resignation, the U.S. Circuit Court of Appeals for the District of Columbia ruled against Nixon on the matter of turning over the tapes.

> **Circuit Court of Appeals:** Though the President is elected by the nationwide ballot, . . . he does not embody the nation's sovereignty. He is not above the law's commands.

FLY ON THE WALL: The court stayed its order for five working days, until October 19, 1973, and urged the president to try to come to some sort of a compromise. Nixon did. He suggested that the White House would give the tapes to Senator John Stennis to listen to. Then Stennis could decide which parts Cox or the Watergate committee could hear. There were two problems with Nixon's proposal: First, Stennis was a Nixon supporter; second, he was hearing impaired.

Cox refused.

SATURDAY NIGHT MASSACRE

Whether we shall continue to be a government of laws and not men is for Congress and ultimately the American people to decide.
—Archibald Cox

FLY ON THE WALL: Even though Richard Nixon was holding on to the tapes, just in case, he ordered his longtime secretary, Rose Mary Woods, to begin transcribing some of them. He asked her not to tell anybody what was on them, but he didn't have to worry about her loyalty.

A friend of Rose Mary Woods: She would die for him. She would just lay down her life for him.

FLY ON THE WALL: As she was transcribing the tape from June 20, 1973, Woods ran into Nixon's office.

FLY ON THE WALL: Woods had accidentally erased part of a tape. Nixon later said he told her not to worry about it. He had just four days to get both Congress and Archibald Cox to agree with his Stennis compromise, which John Stennis hadn't even agreed to. To move things along, Nixon had his men leak (falsely) to reporters that Sam Ervin had happily accepted the Stennis plan.

Ervin: That's outrageous. That's not what I agreed to at all.

FLY ON THE WALL: Cox never accepted the Stennis plan either, even though his refusal to do so put his job at risk.

Cox: I cannot be a party to such an agreement. It is my judgment the President is refusing to comply with the court. . . .

Reporter: Will you resign?

Cox: No. Hell no.

FLY ON THE WALL: This was not the answer Nixon wanted.

Nixon: More than ever, I wanted Cox fired.

FLY ON THE WALL: Sam Dash, the chief counsel on the Ervin Committee, thought Nixon was acting like a king rather than a president.

Dash: Nixon believed that he had absolute unreviewable power to withhold the tapes. He told [Judge Sirica] that the President was as absolute a monarch as Louis XIV had been, but only for 4 years at a time.

FLY ON THE WALL: Beginning on Saturday, October 20, 1973, things really started piling up. Nixon's people ordered Cox to accept the Stennis compromise. Everyone knew he wouldn't, and everyone knew that Nixon would not accept that.

New York Times: All day, newsmen in unusual numbers for a weekend wandered aimlessly through the press area of the White House, waiting for Mr. Cox's news conference . . . and then the president's reaction.

FLY ON THE WALL: Cox kicked things off that Saturday afternoon with a 1:00 P.M. press conference.

Cox: I am certainly not out to get the president of the United States. I am even worried . . . that I am getting too big for my britches, that what I see as principle could be vanity. I hope not. In the end I decided that I had to try to stick by what I thought was right.

FLY ON THE WALL: Minutes after Cox's news conference ended, Attorney General Elliot Richardson got a phone call from Nixon's chief of staff, Alexander Haig.

On orders from your Commander in Chief . . . fire Cox.

Well, I can't do that. . . . I guess I'd better come over to resign.

FLY ON THE WALL: By 4:45 P.M., Richardson was at the White House. Nixon tried bullying Richardson by telling him that he was unpatriotic and might even be endangering world peace.

> **Richardson:** Mr. President, I feel that I have no choice but to go forward [with resigning].

> **Nixon:** Be it on your head.

FLY ON THE WALL: It was now 5:15 P.M. Richardson walked back to his office and told his staff, "The deed is done." The phone rang. This time it was for William D. Ruckelshaus, second in command at the Justice Department.

> **Haig:** You have to obey your Commander in Chief. He has given you an order. Fire Cox.

FLY ON THE WALL: Now it was Ruckelshaus's turn to go see the president and resign. But the Justice Department is filled with lawyers. The third in command was the solicitor general, Robert Bork. The White House sent a limousine and had Bork's orders ready.

> **White House Orders:** Discharge Cox immediately . . . and take all steps necessary to return to the Department of Justice the functions now being performed by the Watergate Special Prosecution force.

FLY ON THE WALL: Bork agreed to the orders and signed off on them. But the day wasn't nearly over. At 8:22 P.M., press secretary Ron Ziegler stood before the crowd of reporters that had gathered.

Ziegler: The President has discharged Cox because he "refused to comply with instructions. . . ." Furthermore, . . . the office of Special Prosecutor was abolished.

FLY ON THE WALL: Every television network interrupted their Saturday-night broadcasts. Newspapers held the presses. As dramatic footage rolled, NBC anchor John Chancellor announced the news.

Chancellor: The country tonight is in the midst of what may be the most serious constitutional crisis in history.

FLY ON THE WALL: Millions were watching when FBI agents arrived at 9:05 P.M. and sealed up the special prosecutor's office. Stunned Justice Department employees stood outside their offices, and some even wept. At 10:00 P.M., Henry S. Ruth Jr., Cox's second in command, came out and—with a pale face and shaky voice—talked to reporters.

Ruth: We all expected something to happen. I guess what I did not expect was to meet an FBI agent who told me I could not take out a love letter from my wife in my office.

FLY ON THE WALL: Historian Fred Emery noted that Nixon's use of political power looked like a coup—a sudden, forceful takeover.

Emery: If Haig had deliberately tried to stage something for the cameras that looked like a coup, he could hardly have done it better.

FLY ON THE WALL: Some Americans took to the streets, others to the phones, to express their shock and anger.

New York Times: By late [that] evening, [October 20, 1973], . . . some public reaction was already visible at the White House. Crowds of young people gathered at the northwest gate. . . . One youth held up a large sign saying, "RESIGN." All evening, the White House switchboard was so swamped with calls that it was almost impossible to get through.

FLY ON THE WALL: What was next?

Time **magazine, November 12, 1973:** Richard Nixon and the nation have passed a tragic point of no return. . . . The nightmare of uncertainty must be ended.

TEETERING ON THE EDGE

People have got to know whether their President
is a crook. Well, I am not a crook.

—Richard Nixon

FLY ON THE WALL: It's hard for people today to imagine how scary the idea of impeachment was in 1973. Given the demonstrations and marches of the 1970s and calls for revolution by some of the protesters at the gates of the White House, many saw impeachment as a threat to America.

> ***Atlanta Constitution*, October 22, 1973:** It is a grave time in American history. The impeachment of a President is a frightening concept.

FLY ON THE WALL: It's one thing to say, "Impeach! Impeach!" But nobody knew what an impeachment would be like. Immediately after what became known as the Saturday Night Massacre, twenty bills of impeachment were introduced, including one by the Congressional Black Caucus.

> **New York Times, October 25, 1973:** In a statement, . . . the Congressional Black Caucus urged examination of what it called a "cascade" of "executive crimes."

FLY ON THE WALL: Poked enough, the House of Representatives—the congressional body responsible for starting impeachment proceedings—had to actually do something. They chose Peter Rodino, a representative from New Jersey who had recently become chairman of the House Judiciary Committee, to oversee the impeachment process. However, as noted by influential columnist Jimmy Breslin, Rodino was not the boldest member of Congress.

> **Breslin:** [Rodino] exhibited a great natural cautiousness.

FLY ON THE WALL: Historian Fred Emery described the scene in Congress the week following the Saturday Night Massacre.

> **Emery:** When Congress reconvened on Tuesday morning, formal preparations for impeachment proceeded. In

the first 45 minutes of the session, not a single Republican rose to support Richard Nixon.

FLY ON THE WALL: Three hours after Congress voted to begin impeachment hearings, Nixon's lawyer Charles Wright was at Judge John J. Sirica's door.

> **Wright:** The President of the United States will comply in all respects.

FLY ON THE WALL: That meant Nixon was going to release his tapes to Congress. Everyone was stunned.

> **Wright (virtuously):** This President does not defy the law.

FLY ON THE WALL: That was tricky. The whole world had just watched Nixon defy the law forty-eight hours earlier by firing Archibald Cox. Nixon was trying to do a 180-degree turn. This was the beginning of "Operation Candor," as recalled by *New York Times* reporter J. Anthony Lukas.

> **Lukas:** It was a new phase in the Watergate saga—a period in which the President tried to give the impression that he was bowing to the courts, cooperating with the investigators, and speaking candidly to the public.

FLY ON THE WALL: Nixon was hopeful that his noble gesture of cooperation would be enough to quiet the calls for impeachment. But Rodino wasn't buying it.

New York Times, October 25, 1973: Rodino said . . . "[We will] proceed full steam ahead" with the impeachment investigation despite the president's sudden decision yesterday to surrender the Watergate tapes to the courts.

FLY ON THE WALL: To launch Operation Candor, Nixon gave a press conference. He wasn't good at candor.

Nixon: I have never heard or seen such outrageous, vicious, distorted reporting in twenty-seven years of public life. . . . [The nation has been] pounded night after night with . . . frantic, hysterical reporting.

FLY ON THE WALL: Nixon fought to get control of his temper and tried again.

Don't get the impression that you arouse my anger. You see, one can only be angry with those he respects.

FLY ON THE WALL: Most reporters could barely keep a straight face, and a lot of the nation was also laughing at the president. Then things got even worse. Just one week after his lawyer had said so virtuously that Nixon did not defy the law, Sirica announced that two of the tapes he had asked for were missing. Republican senator Mark Hatfield, from Oregon, came close to calling Nixon a liar.

Hatfield: The startling revelation that certain key tapes of the President's conversations do not exist—the very tapes that have been fought over to the brink of a constitutional crisis—dramatically escalates the problems of the administration's credibility.

FLY ON THE WALL: Still, Nixon wasn't ready to give up on Operation Candor. His staff arranged a tour through the South, where he was still popular. But luck was not on Nixon's side. In Orlando, Florida, just before he was set to make a big speech at Disney World, along came another bombshell: For two years, as president, Nixon had paid almost no taxes, even though he earned over $200,000 a year.

Nixon: People have got to know whether their President is a crook. Well, I am not a crook.

FLY ON THE WALL: Once again, Operation Candor flopped. The statement "I am not a crook" soon became the most quoted five words of the Watergate era. Comedian Jon Stewart, then a child, was one of many who recognized the absurdity of the president's words.

Stewart: I was only ten years old and I killed with my Nixon "I Am Not a Crook" impersonation.

FLY ON THE WALL: A few days later, Nixon met with Republican governors from across the country, including Tom McCall, governor of Oregon.

> **McCall (anxiously):** Are we going to be blindsided by more bombshells?

> **Nixon:** If there are any more bombs, I am not aware of them.

FLY ON THE WALL: Nixon was lying. He knew that the very next day his lawyers were due in court. This time they had to explain the eighteen-and-a-half-minute gap in the June 20, 1972, tape, the one that Rose Mary Woods erased and also the one where Nixon first told Bob Haldeman to lie to the CIA to get them to take the blame for Watergate.

> ***New York Times:*** President Nixon's personal secretary erased a key 18-minute segment of one of the most important Watergate tapes: a tape between Richard Nixon and H. R. Haldeman, his Chief of Staff, three days after the break-in. [The White House said it was "inadvertent."] A Washington audio technician with long experience in tape recordings said it would be very difficult to wipe out such a long passage by mistake.

FLY ON THE WALL: Sirica insisted on an open-court hearing. Prosecutor Jill Volner asked Woods to demonstrate how she erased the tape. The secretary tried to show how she reached for the phone and took her foot off the pedal of the transcription

machine—a pose that became known as the "Rose Mary Stretch" when the press printed a photo of her doing it. Eventually, experts decided that the eighteen-and-a-half-minute gap could not have been caused the way that she said. In truth, the gap had been caused by somewhere between five and nine separate "accidents"; in other words, someone did it on purpose.

Sirica: [The gap in the tape] . . . leads to a distinct possibility of unlawful conduct on the part of one or more persons.

FLY ON THE WALL: Senator Charles Mathias, a Republican from Maryland, expressed his opinion in a statement to the press.

Mathias: I think the alternatives to impeachment become less and less.

LULL BEFORE THE SUPREME STORM

There is a time to fly . . . and there is a time to fight, and I'm going to fight like hell.

—Richard Nixon

FLY ON THE WALL: The public got to rest from Watergate over the Christmas holidays. They needed the break from bombshell after bombshell. But there was no rest for Richard Nixon. The people who cared about Nixon, such as his daughter Julie, were worried.

Julie Nixon Eisenhower: My father was more tense and uncommunicative than I ever remembered him. He had withdrawn into his own world and away from his family.

FLY ON THE WALL: There were rumors that he was drinking too much, that he was unhinged, playing the piano in the dark in the White House. Chuck Colson, still serving as special counsel to the president, recalled a bleak holiday.

Colson: The White House Christmas party that year was a wake. Never have I seen liquor flow more freely and produce fewer smiles.

FLY ON THE WALL: Nixon had plenty of ghosts to deal with: all those failures. But a note he wrote at 1:15 A.M. on New Year's Day 1974 suggests that he wasn't ready to give up.

Nixon (writing to himself): Do I fight all out, or do I now begin the long process [toward] resignation? The Answer: FIGHT. . . . Act like a president . . . act like a winner. Opponents are savage destroyers, haters. Time to use full power of the President to fight.

FLY ON THE WALL: Of course, we don't really know what Nixon thought. We know what he says he thought, but Nixon was not famous for his honesty. Still, we can be pretty sure that the worry was getting to him.

> **Nixon:** The biggest danger I saw in the year ahead was that both the Special Prosecutor and the House Judiciary Committee would begin requesting more and more tapes.

FLY ON THE WALL: Nixon's newest problem was a man named Leon Jaworski, who had replaced Archibald Cox as special prosecutor. Jaworski was from Texas, and he had been chairman of the Texas Democrats for Nixon. The lawyers and investigators who had worked for Cox were afraid that Jaworski wasn't willing to fight the way Cox had. But then Jaworski listened to one of the tapes.

> **Nixon (on tape, to Bob Haldeman, who was preparing to testify):** Just be damned sure you say, "I don't remember, I can't recall. . . ."

> **Jaworski (to jury):** Can you imagine that? The president of the United States sitting in his office telling his staff how to commit perjury?

FLY ON THE WALL: On February 6, 1974, the House passed a resolution, by a vote of 410 to 4, to launch an official impeachment inquiry. On March 1, Bob Haldeman, John Mitchell, John Ehrlichman, and Chuck Colson were indicted by a federal grand jury. Jaworski was in charge of their prosecution, and he immediately demanded sixty-four more tapes, from days he knew were important. Remember that, at the time, nobody knew that there were actually 3,700 hours of tapes. The House Judiciary Committee wanted some of the same tapes, too. Once again, Nixon refused, and his press secretary, Ron Ziegler, used a vivid analogy to explain the president's position.

> **Ziegler:** The mere fact of an impeachment inquiry does not give Congress the right to back up a truck and haul off White House files.

FLY ON THE WALL: Actually, it does. That was exactly what the impeachment hearings meant. The House had the responsibility to decide if there should be charges. The representatives' position was that they could look at everything. Nixon decided he would give them edited versions of the tape transcripts. He decided he'd better edit the transcripts himself. He took out his swear words, replacing them with the phrase "[expletive deleted]." He explained that the salty language on the tapes would have upset his mother. Fred Buzhardt, one of Nixon's lawyers, admitted that Nixon swore like the devil.

> **Buzhardt:** You know how he talks in the Oval Office; you would think he was Beelzebub reincarnated.

Oh, **EXPLETIVE DELETED** AND FURTHERMORE **EXPLETIVE DELETED**

FLY ON THE WALL: On April 29, 1974, Nixon went on TV again. His desk was stacked with black binders: 1,300 pages of transcripts, which actually was a mere drop in the bucket.

Nixon: The president has nothing to hide. . . . Everything that is relevant is included, the rough as well as the smooth. . . . These transcripts will provide grist for many sensational stories in the press. . . . They will embarrass me. . . . [But] because this is an issue that profoundly affects all the American people, . . . I have directed that they should all be made public.

FLY ON THE WALL: The price for the public to purchase the 1,300 pages was $13.25. In one week, the transcripts sold more than three million copies. People started using the phrase "expletive deleted" all the time.

> **Q.** Why did the chicken cross the road?

> **A.** Because it [expletive deleted] wanted to.

FLY ON THE WALL: But, for many people, such as popular televangelist Billy Graham, there was nothing funny about reading the transcripts.

> **Graham:** I felt like throwing up.

FLY ON THE WALL: Language aside, investigators were not willing to accept Nixon's versions of the truth. James Doyle, a journalist who worked as an investigator for both Cox and Jaworski, summed up their feelings.

> **Doyle:** The White House gambit of releasing the transcripts surpassed even the firing of Archibald Cox as a measure of desperation. The shock and outrage . . . [grew] greater each day . . . as more and more read more and more pages. The Nixon administration had lost its last shred of self-respect.

FLY ON THE WALL: Nixon didn't even gain anything by releasing his versions of the tapes. The committee voted 20–18 to reject the transcripts. The chair of the House Judiciary Committee, Peter Rodino, expressed the majority's feelings in sharp words.

Rodino: We did not subpoena an edited White House version of partial transcripts. We did not subpoena a presidential interpretation of what is necessary and relevant evidence.

FLY ON THE WALL: Jaworski asked the Supreme Court to hear the case as quickly as possible. The Supreme Court agreed. The arguments in *United States v. Richard Milhous Nixon* were set to begin on July 8, 1974.

DYING BY INCHES

**We are dying by inches. . . . Our margin for error
has disappeared; our reservoir of credibility
with the American people dried up.**
—Patrick Buchanan to Richard Nixon

FLY ON THE WALL: The summer of 1974 looked a lot like
a duck. On the surface, it was hardly moving, but under-
neath, webbed feet were paddling like crazy. Behind closed
doors, investigators and prosecutors were assembling their
ammunition and arguments, and so were the White House
lawyers.

***Miami Herald*, August 7, 1974:** We think the end is

near. Not for the republic, which is basically sound, but for Richard Milhous Nixon. . . . He [should] accept resignation. . . . That will be the expedient thing to do . . . and Richard Nixon has always done the expedient.

FLY ON THE WALL: Nixon's problem at this point was figuring out what was expedient. Historian John Farrell has described his efforts.

> **Farrell:** He took out a pad of paper and began listing the pros and cons of resigning. The idea of quitting was horrid to him. He had built a whole persona around never quitting.

FLY ON THE WALL: The president had one hope left. He argued that the House of Representatives could not impeach him unless they had clear proof that he had committed a specific crime. Once more, everyone was glued to their television. On July 24, 1974, it was Peter Rodino's turn to bang down the gavel.

> **Rodino:** Our judgment is not concerned with an individual but with a system of constitutional government.

FLY ON THE WALL: Barbara Jordan, a congresswoman from Texas, became a star of the House hearings. She began her speech by reminding her listeners that when the Constitution was written, she was not included in the phrase "We the people" because she was a woman and she was black, and she ended it with a stirring call for impeachment.

Today I am an inquisitor. I believe hyperbole would not be fictional and would not overstate the solemnness that I feel right now. My faith in the Constitution is whole, it is complete, it is total. I am not going to sit here and be an idle spectator to the diminution, the subversion, the destruction of the Constitution. . . . The framers confined in the Congress the power, if need be, to remove the President in order to strike a delicate balance between a President swollen with power and grown tyrannical, and the preservation of the independence of the executive.

FLY ON THE WALL: When the Constitution was written, the framers wanted to make sure that we were citizens of a society, not subjects of a king. Jordan wanted everyone to understand that it was the Constitution that held us together, not a king or a president. Peaceful transition of power has always been a source of pride for Americans. That is the thing which is most admired by others about American politics. That's why even though the impeachment clause is in the Constitution, it has been very rarely used. Impeachment was to be used only in case of an emergency. This was an emergency.

> **Jordan:** If the impeachment provision in the Constitution of the United States will not reach the offenses charged here, then perhaps the eighteenth-century Constitution should be abandoned to a twentieth-century paper shredder!

FLY ON THE WALL: Still, not everyone was willing to put Nixon's presidency into the shredder.

> ***Manchester Union Leader*, July 30, 1974:** Anyone watching the televised operations of the Judiciary Committee could only be reminded of a group of vultures—in Nevada we call them buzzards, circling around the sky—over a wounded animal. A great many of the committee members looked as if they would make the heart of a buzzard appear mild and loving in comparison to theirs.

FLY ON THE WALL: Nixon watched things unravel from his home in California. He was hiding, actually. During the months of June and July, he spent fewer than six days in the White House.

> **Nixon:** Lowest point in the presidency, and Supreme Court still to come.

FLY ON THE WALL: But Nixon hadn't touched bottom yet—not nearly. The day of the argument before the Supreme Court, July 8, 1974, was hot and muggy. People had been up all night for a chance to see history being made. Nixon was hoping that the court would accept the argument that only the president could decide what was covered by executive privilege. Political journalist Elizabeth Drew's description of that day reflected what those in attendance must have felt.

> **Drew:** Inside this building, with its marble hallways, there is a special coolness. . . . It is as if this were a sort of temple. . . . We have come to think of this court as the guarantor of our safety, as the last refuge when other remedies fail.

FLY ON THE WALL: As the case proceeded, Justice Lewis F. Powell raised the question of whether the president was allowed to cover up a crime. The White House, represented by Nixon's special counsel James St. Clair, gave an answer that bordered on nonsense.

> **Powell:** What public interest is there in preserving secrecy with respect to a criminal conspiracy?

> **St. Clair:** The answer, sir, is that a criminal conspiracy is criminal only after it's proven to be criminal.

FLY ON THE WALL: You don't need to be a judge to recognize gobbledygook. Chief Justice Warren Burger easily shot down Nixon's lawyers' argument that only the president can decide what is covered by executive privilege.

Burger: Presidential privilege does not mean all material in the possession of a president is immune in all circumstances.

FLY ON THE WALL: The decision, which came on July 24, 1974, less than three weeks after the argument, was brief and shocking. The court ordered the president to release the tapes by a vote of 8–0. It was James Doyle, the investigator for the special prosecutors, who gave a summary of Nixon's reaction.

Doyle: The President considered defying the high court, and some of his aides considered having Nixon destroy the evidence and resign, claiming that he was doing so to protect the integrity of presidential files.

FLY ON THE WALL: On July 27, 1974, the House Committee voted 27–11 for impeachment. Nixon had gone swimming on the beach near his house in California and was changing into dry clothes when press secretary Ron Ziegler called him.

Nixon: That was how I learned that I was the first president in 106 years to be recommended for impeachment, standing in the beach trailer, barefoot, . . . [wearing a] blue windbreaker emblazoned with the Presidential Seal.

BACK TO CALIFORNIA

**To leave office before my term is completed is
abhorrent to every instinct in my body. But, as
president, I must put the interests of America first.**
—Richard Nixon

FLY ON THE WALL: Richard Nixon now had his back truly
against the wall. The House was going to impeach him, and the
criminal prosecution and Congress—in fact, all the world—got
to hear the tape from June 23, 1972, in which Nixon made it clear
he knew about the break-in. That tape became known as the
"smoking gun." The phrase goes all the way back to a Sherlock
Holmes story, but it became forever connected to Watergate as
the one thing that proved the president not only had lied but had

actually done something criminal. John Dean understood that the end was near.

Dean: When the smoking gun was released, [Nixon's] loyal supporters, both on the White House staff and throughout government and the news media, discovered that they had been lied to by the president and could no longer support him.

FLY ON THE WALL: Nixon finally came clean.

***New York Times*, August 6, 1974:** In a sharp setback to his fight against impeachment, President Nixon admitted today that six days after the Watergate burglary, he ordered a halt to the investigation of the break-in . . . and that he kept the evidence from his lawyers and supporters.

FLY ON THE WALL: Republicans in Congress were furious.

Robert McClory, R-IL: Any delay now is only a question of his personal stubbornness and personal stonewalling.

FLY ON THE WALL: Nixon had always liked poker. He was willing to try one last bluff. The House could impeach him, but that meant nothing unless the Senate voted to convict him. On August 6 he told his cabinet that he would *not* resign. That scared his family, the people closest to him. They knew he was sleeping too little and drinking too much.

His daughter Tricia's husband, Edward Cox (who was not related, by the way, to Archibald Cox), noted that the president was sometimes acting unstable.

Edward Cox: The President was up walking the halls last night, talking to pictures of former Presidents— giving speeches and talking to the pictures on the wall.

FLY ON THE WALL: They were nervous at the Pentagon, too. After all, Nixon still controlled the military and had his finger on the "button" that could trigger a nuclear attack. In an extraordinary move, the secretary of defense informed the joint chiefs of the military forces that orders from Nixon should no longer be automatically obeyed.

> **Defense Secretary James Schlesinger issued an unprecedented set of orders:** If the president gave any nuclear launch order, military commanders should check with either him [Schlesinger] or Secretary of State Henry Kissinger before executing them. Schlesinger feared that the president, who seemed depressed and was drinking heavily, might order Armageddon. . . . Senator Alan Cranston [warned] about "the need for keeping a berserk president from plunging us into a holocaust."

FLY ON THE WALL: While everyone was nervously waiting for Nixon to make his next move, and hoping for his resignation, the women in Nixon's family never lost faith in him—not Pat, and not his daughters, Tricia and Julie.

> **Julie Nixon Eisenhower (in a letter):** Dear Daddy. I love you. Whatever you do I will support. I am very proud of you. Please wait a week or even ten days before you make this decision. Go through the fire just a little bit longer. . . . You are so strong. I love you. . . . Millions support you.

FLY ON THE WALL: Millions did support him, but many more millions did not—especially the Republicans in Congress. On August 7, three Senate Republican leaders, including Hugh Scott of Pennsylvania, went to tell him that if the impeachment proceeded to trial, which was certain, Nixon would lose in the Senate.

Scott: We told him the situation is very gloomy on Capitol Hill.

FLY ON THE WALL: Another of those senators was Barry Goldwater of Arizona.

Goldwater: Yes, sir. . . . There aren't many who would support you. . . . I couldn't find more than four firm votes.

Nixon: Never mind. There'll be no tears.

FLY ON THE WALL: Even after the senators left, still nobody knew what Nixon would do.

New York Times **(August 8, 1974):** The official White House position . . . was that the President would not resign, but would ride out the impeachment process to the end.

FLY ON THE WALL: But in truth, by the end of that day, Nixon had made up his mind for good. He would resign.

Nixon (to his family): We're going back to California.

FLY ON THE WALL: Just then, the White House photographer knocked on the door. Julie and Tricia were in tears. Pat Nixon told the photographer to go away, but the president stopped him.

Nixon: Oh, come on, take a few shots.

FLY ON THE WALL: Nixon even arranged where they would stand. Pat Nixon always hated the photograph.

Pat Nixon: Our hearts were breaking, and there we are smiling.

FLY ON THE WALL: After the photographer and Nixon's family left, Nixon was on his own.

Nixon: I went to . . . work on my resignation speech. . . . I could even feel a kind of calm starting to settle in.

FLY ON THE WALL: There was a press briefing the next day.

New York Times, August 9, 1974: At 12:30 this afternoon, the White House Press Secretary, Ronald L. Ziegler, announced that the President would address the nation at 9 p.m. Mr. Ziegler did not say what the speech would be about. He did not have to. He choked on his words several times and was struggling visibly to keep himself under control as he left the rostrum of the packed but hushed briefing room at the White House.

FLY ON THE WALL: Steven Bull, Nixon's personal aide and appointments secretary, gave his view on the president's state of mind.

Bull: Yesterday I saw a degree of anguish. Today there is an acceptance of whatever it is he is going to do.

FLY ON THE WALL: *New York Times* reporter J. Anthony Lukas described the scene that evening.

Lukas: Outside the White House, at the gates, crowds gathered on the sidewalk, standing three, four, five deep, their faces pressed against the iron fence in a kind of deathwatch.

James J. Johnson, of Baltimore, who joined the crowd: It's a historic moment, something you ain't gonna see too much in a lifetime.

FLY ON THE WALL: Some in the crowd began singing "God Bless America" as the time drew near for Nixon's speech.

Nixon (to Bull, explaining his tears): I've got a little bit of a cold. The sniffles or something.

FLY ON THE WALL: But by the time Nixon was ready to go before the television cameras, he got himself under control, even joking with the cameramen.

Nixon: Blonds, they say, photograph better than brunettes. Is that true or not?

FLY ON THE WALL: At 9:01 P.M. on August 8, 1974, Richard Nixon sat in his chair in the Oval Office and looked straight into the camera.

Nixon: Good evening, this is the thirty-seventh time I have spoken to you from this office. . . . In the past few days . . . it has become evident to me that I no longer have a strong enough political base. . . . There is no longer a need for the process to be prolonged. I would have preferred to carry through to the finish. . . . I have never been a quitter. To leave office before my term is completed is abhorrent to every instinct in my body. But, as president, I must put the interests of America first. . . .

Therefore, I shall resign the presidency effective at noon tomorrow. . . . In leaving it, I do so with this prayer: May God's grace be with you in all the days ahead.

FLY ON THE WALL: This was the first time that a president of the United States had ever resigned. According to law, the president resigns to the secretary of state. His resignation letter, addressed to Secretary of State Henry Kissinger, contained a single sentence.

August 9, 1974
Dear Mr. Secretary:

I hereby resign the Office of President of the United States.

Sincerely,
Richard Nixon

FLY ON THE WALL: No longer president, Nixon addressed the members of his cabinet and the White House staff later that day.

Nixon (in the East Room of the White House, with his family by his side): We think that when someone dear to us dies, we think that when we lose an election, we think that when we suffer a defeat, that all is ended. . . . Not true. It is only a beginning, always. The young must know it; the old must know it. It must always sustain us, because the greatness comes not when things go always good for you, but the greatness comes, and you are really tested, when you take some knocks, some disappointments, when sadness comes, because only if you have been in the deepest valley can you ever know how magnificent it is to be on the highest mountain. . . . Always remember, others may hate you, but those who hate you don't win unless you hate them, and then you destroy yourself. And so, we leave with high hopes, in good spirit, and with deep humility, and with very much gratefulness in our hearts.

FLY ON THE WALL: With that, Nixon departed from the south side of the White House and climbed the stairs to the presidential helicopter. At the top he turned, waved, and raised his arms high, smiling and making a "V" with each hand in his trademark victory stance.

And then he was gone.

Minutes later, Vice President Gerald R. Ford was sworn in as the thirty-eighth president of the United States.

Ford: My fellow Americans, our long national nightmare is over. Our Constitution works.

I GAVE THEM A SWORD AND THEY STUCK IT IN

I gave them a sword and they stuck it in.
And I guess if I'd been in their position
I'd have done the same thing.

—Richard Nixon

FLY ON THE WALL: Richard Nixon went back to San Clemente, California. He had a nice house there on the ocean, with a swimming pool and a three-hole golf course. Back in Washington, John Dean, whose house did not overlook the ocean, packed his bags to go to jail. There were no more crisp hundred-dollar bills to pay for lawyers.

> **Dean:** I was spread-eagled against the wall in the cellblock beneath the courthouse, frisked, fingerprinted and then posed for mug shots. . . . Down the hall into a cell. A huge door clanged shut behind me.

FLY ON THE WALL: Then, on September 8, 1974, President Gerald Ford granted Nixon a full and unconditional pardon.

> **Ford:** [It] is an American tragedy in which we all have played a part. It could go on and on and on, or someone must write the end to it. I have concluded that only I can do that, and if I can, I must.

FLY ON THE WALL: Archibald Cox, the special prosecutor Nixon had fired, disapproved of the pardon and looked back on it years later with harsh words.

> **Cox:** The pardon violated the principle that all individuals, powerful and powerless, rich and poor, must stand equally at the bar of justice.

FLY ON THE WALL: Carl Bernstein and Bob Woodward, the *Washington Post* reporters who had worked so hard to bring the events of the Watergate scandal to light, had even harsher words.

Bernstein (to Woodward at the time of the pardon): The son of a bitch pardoned the son of a bitch.

FLY ON THE WALL: Bob Haldeman and John Ehrlichman both asked for pardons but did not receive them. In fact, none of the men who went to jail for Nixon received pardons. Meanwhile, pardon in hand, the former president soon signed a $2.5 million contract for his memoirs. Journalist Elizabeth Drew called the memoirs something else.

Drew: He drew up a secret plan . . . to regain respectability. It was given the code name Wizard.

FLY ON THE WALL: Money just kept rolling in for Nixon, which was lucky because he had enormous expenses—being impeached meant having to pay a great deal in legal fees. In 1977, Nixon signed a $600,000 deal to be interviewed by TV journalist David Frost. Over forty million people watched.

Nixon to Frost, May 19, 1977: Well, when the president does it, that means that it is not illegal.

FLY ON THE WALL: Frost posed difficult questions, but Nixon was a pro at ducking and dodging. This battling back and forth went on for seven days until Frost finally lost it.

Frost: Admit Watergate was probably more than mistakes. . . . There was wrongdoing. . . . (Say) "I put the American people through two years of needless agony and I apologize for that."

FLY ON THE WALL: But Nixon saw it differently.

Nixon: Most of all, I let down an opportunity that I would have had for two and a half more years for building a lasting peace.

FLY ON THE WALL: Nixon seemed to miss the point about an apology.

Nixon: If they want me to get down and grovel on the floor, no. Never. Because I don't believe I should. But I brought myself down. I gave them a sword and they stuck it in. And I guess if I'd been in their position I'd have done the same thing.

FLY ON THE WALL: Nixon lived another twenty years. He wrote nine books that all concentrated on making himself respectable, a great president, even. He died, following a stroke, on April 22, 1994, at the age of eighty-one. Over four thousand people attended his funeral, including all the living presidents and over one hundred members of Congress. Nixon was given a full military burial on his father's lemon farm, which at that point had become the Nixon Presidential Library. The police estimated that fifty thousand people waited in line for eighteen hours to pay their respects. On the day of his funeral, a reporter from New York City spoke to some students at the college where one of the authors of this book was teaching.

Reporter: What do you know about Richard Nixon?

Student: Why is everybody making such a fuss? I thought he was a crook.

FLY ON THE WALL: Maybe he was. But he was many other things as well. One of them was that he was the thirty-seventh president of the United States—and that matters.

EPILOGUE

The year of the Watergate break-in should have been a glorious year for Richard Nixon. In 1972, he was running for reelection for his second term as president, and he had a huge lead in the polls. He had accomplished a lot of things in his first term. He was the first U.S. president to visit Communist China. He negotiated a historic antinuclear treaty with the Soviet Union. He established the Environmental Protection Agency (EPA) and signed the Clean Air Act. But with all that, Watergate is what most people think of when they hear his name.

The Watergate story has many heroes, along with its villains. Investigative journalists acted as sleuths, and their bosses were not afraid to publish their stories. Judges heard hard cases and made hard decisions, forcing a sitting president to reveal secret tapes. A few honorable members of Nixon's administration refused to participate in the cover-up. Members of Nixon's own party courageously risked their political careers by contemplating the impeachment of a president who had been reelected by a landslide.

We like to see Watergate as the success of the system of checks and balances we celebrate in the U.S. Constitution. But there is another, darker side to the legacy of Watergate. The cynicism and skepticism of our current political culture has its roots in the years of the Nixon scandals.

Every quote we have used in this book comes from a documented source. There is a difference between the words that people actually say and what other people say those words mean. In history, we call this the difference between primary and secondary sources. Primary sources can tell us a lot—through the words that people spoke and wrote. But people lie. And there are some things that we don't know—and we can never know.

People often tell historians how lucky they are that they don't have to keep up with new material since history doesn't change. They are wrong. Tapes are still being transcribed, and new materials keep popping up. That changes how we understand the past. And it's not just the new materials that changes history; it's also what's happening around us. The past doesn't change, but how we understand it certainly does.

People who love history recognize that there are things we cannot know. That's why people keep writing and thinking about the people and actions in the past. They're trying to figure it out.

History is shaped by when you start the story and when you end it. For the people who lived through Watergate and were close to it, the ending pleased no one. Perhaps the words of the two biggest players on this stage are one way for us to end.

Archibald Cox (the special prosecutor fired during the Saturday Night Massacre): The Watergate affair . . . marked two national crises in the use or abuse of political power. One was moral: what standards of honour and decency would the public conscience impose . . . ? [The second was]: how deep is the attachment of the people to constitutionalism and how great is their moral and political power to enforce it?

Richard Nixon (speaking to his aides who followed him to California shortly after he had to resign in disgrace): What starts the process, really, are the laughs and slights and snubs when you are a kid. . . . But if you are reasonably intelligent and if your anger is deep enough and strong enough, you learn that you can change those attitudes by excellence, personal gut performance, while those who have everything are sitting on their fat butts. Once you learn that you've got to work harder than everybody else, it becomes a way of life as you move out of the alley and on your way. . . . In your mind, you have nothing to lose, so you take plenty of chances. . . . It's a piece of cake until you get to the top. . . . [Then] you find you can't stop playing the game the way you've always played it because it is part of you and you need it. . . . So you . . . walk on the edge of the precipice because over the years you have become fascinated by how close to the edge you can walk. . . . This time there was a difference. This time we had something to lose.

John Dean

John Ehrlichman

H. R. (Bob) Haldeman

E. Howard Hunt

G. Gordon Liddy

James McCord

John Mitchell

Charles (Chuck) Colson

Jeb Magruder

WHERE THEY ARE NOW: PEOPLE WHO WENT TO JAIL

John Dean (October 14, 1938–): Dean pleaded guilty to conspiracy to obstruct justice and was sentenced to one to four years in prison. He served only four months because he was cooperating with the prosecutors. On his release from prison, he wrote several tell-all books. His first was *Blind Ambition* (1976), followed by *Lost Honor* (1982). Then came *Worse Than Watergate* (2004), about George W. Bush and the deception leading to the Iraq War. In 2014, he wrote *The Nixon Defense: What He Knew and When He Knew It* using the latest revelations from the Nixon Tapes. Disbarred from practicing law, Dean became an investment banker and frequent commentator (a "talking head") on television. He is still married to Mo.

John Ehrlichman (March 20, 1925–February 14, 1999): Ehrlichman was convicted of perjury and sentenced to two and a half to eight years in prison. He served eighteen months. After his release from prison, he wrote a book on the scandal, *Witness to Power: The Nixon Years* (1982), and then went on to write several novels. Ehrlichman wrote, "I don't miss Richard Nixon very much. Richard Nixon probably doesn't much miss me either."

H. R. (Bob) Haldeman (October 27, 1926–November 12, 1993): Haldeman was sentenced to two and a half to eight years in prison for conspiracy and obstruction of justice. He served eighteen months in the Lompoc federal prison in California. While there, he worked in the sewage treatment facility. His book on Watergate, *The Ends of Power*, was published in 1978. Until the end of his life, Haldeman maintained that he was innocent. A version of his diaries was published the year after his death.

E. Howard Hunt (October 9, 1918–January 23, 2007): Hunt was convicted of burglary, conspiracy, and wiretapping. He spent thirty-three months at the federal correctional complex in Allenwood, Pennsylvania. After Nixon was pardoned, Hunt applied for a pardon, too, but was turned down. While in prison he had a stroke. Paroled in 1977, he moved to Florida and started a new family. At the time of his death, he was working on his memoir, *American Spy: My Secret History in the CIA, Watergate, and Beyond*. It was published posthumously in 2007.

G. Gordon Liddy (November 30, 1930–): Liddy was convicted of burglary, conspiracy, and wiretapping. He spent four and a half years in prison. After his release, he wrote a book about Watergate, an autobiography called *Will* (1980). It was a best-seller. He played both himself and various G-men (that is, FBI agents) on several TV shows. He hosted a radio show until 2012. As of 2018, he had a website called The G. Man Club.

James McCord (June 16, 1924–2017): McCord was convicted on eight counts of conspiracy, burglary, and wiretapping. He served just eighty-two days in prison and was paroled because of his cooperation and the letter he wrote to Judge John J. Sirica. His book on Watergate is *A Piece of Tape: The Watergate Story— Fact and Fiction* (1974).

John Mitchell (September 15, 1913–November 9, 1988): After his indictment, Mitchell moved out of his Watergate apartment and filed for divorce from Martha. He was convicted for perjury, conspiracy, and obstruction of justice and sentenced to one to four years in prison. After hearing his sentence, he remarked, "It could have been worse. They could have sentenced me to spend the rest of my life with Martha Mitchell." He was paroled for medical reasons after a year and a half in jail. When he died in 1988, he was buried with full military honors.

Charles (Chuck) Colson (October 16, 1931–April 21, 2012): Colson pleaded guilty to obstruction of justice and was sentenced to one to three years in prison. Soon after arriving in prison he became an Evangelical Christian, preaching to his fellow prisoners, including John Dean and Jeb Magruder. For the rest of his life, Colson was a minister and worked for prison reform. He did not write a book about Watergate, but his book *Born Again* (1976) told his story and was made into a movie.

Jeb Magruder (November 5, 1934–May 11, 2014): Magruder pleaded guilty and was sentenced to prison for four years. He served seven months in the federal correctional complex in Allenwood, Pennsylvania. While in jail, he became a minister; after his release, he attended divinity school. His book on Watergate, *An American Life: One Man's Road to Watergate*, was published in 1974. The mayor of Columbus, Ohio, appointed Magruder chairman of a commission on values and ethics. In an interview, Magruder was asked if his values had changed for the better after prison. "If they haven't changed," he said, "then it has been a real waste of time, hasn't it?" In 2008, he pleaded guilty to reckless driving after he plowed into a motorcycle and a truck. His license was suspended.

WHERE THEY ARE NOW: THE PEOPLE WHO PUT THE PEOPLE IN JAIL

Archibald Cox (May 17, 1912–May 29, 2004): After Watergate, Cox returned to Harvard Law School and had a distinguished career. On January 8, 2001, President Bill Clinton presented Cox with the President's Citizen Medal, saying, "Every American . . . owes you a profound debt of thanks . . . for a lifetime of service to your country and its Constitution."

Sam Ervin (September 27, 1896–April 23, 1985): Ervin retired from the Senate shortly after Watergate. In 1973, he recorded a music album, *Senator Sam at Home*, which included Ervin singing "Bridge over Troubled Water." He wrote *The Whole Truth: The Watergate Conspiracy* (1980) and *Humor of a Country Lawyer* (1983). In 2001, he became the subject of a one-man play, *Senator Sam*, by North Carolina journalist Steve Bouser.

Bob Woodward (March 26, 1942–): Woodward continues to write books and to work as a reporter for the *Washington Post*. Right after Watergate, Woodward and Carl Bernstein published two bestsellers on Watergate, *All the President's Men* (1974) and *The Final Days* (1976). In 1976, *All the President's Men* was made into a movie (with Robert Redford playing Woodward) that won many awards, including four Oscars. Woodward is often seen on television as a commentator. In 2018, he released a segment for the online education platform MasterClass: Bob Woodward Teaches Investigative Journalism. He also released another bestseller, this time about a different president, Donald Trump, called *Fear* (2018).

Carl Bernstein (February 14, 1944–): Bernstein, like Woodward, continues to work as an investigative journalist; he is a commentator on the use and abuse of power for CNN. Dustin Hoffman played him in the 1976 movie *All the President's Men*.

TIMELINE

1971

February 16: President Richard Nixon hires technicians to secretly install automatic recording equipment in the Oval Office, the President's Executive Office, the Cabinet Room, and the Lincoln Sitting Room.

June 13: The *New York Times* publishes the first installment of the Pentagon Papers, leaked by Daniel Ellsberg.

July 24: Nixon creates the Special Investigations Unit, which becomes known as "the plumbers." Its members include G. Gordon Liddy, E. Howard Hunt, and James McCord.

September 9: Hunt, Liddy, and a team of burglars break into Ellsberg's psychiatrist's office to look for dirt on Ellsberg.

September 9: Nixon aides begin compiling the Enemies List.

1972

January 27: Liddy first presents Operation Gemstone, outlining "black bag" jobs.

February 4: Liddy slightly scales back his plan for illegal activities.

March 1: John Mitchell resigns as attorney general to become head of the Committee to Re-Elect the President (CREEP).

May 28: The plumbers attempt to break into the Democratic National Committee headquarters at the Watergate complex to bug the telephones. One bug doesn't work.

June 17: The plumbers go back to fix the broken bug and are arrested at 2:30 A.M. with cameras, eavesdropping equipment, and $2,300 in cash, mostly $100 bills.

June 17: A *Washington Post* story asserts that one of the burglars caught at the Watergate had the names and numbers of top Nixon aides in his address book.

June 20: The first conversation about Watergate between Nixon and Bob Haldeman is recorded. (This tape contains the eighteen-and-a-half-minute gap that came to light in the later hearings.)

June 23: Haldeman and Nixon are recorded talking about covering up their involvement in Watergate. (The recording later becomes known as the "smoking gun" tape.)

July 1: Mitchell resigns as head of CREEP.

August 30: Nixon announces that White House counsel John Dean has investigated the break-in and nobody in the White House staff played any part. (Untrue!)

September 15: The Watergate burglars are indicted.

October 10: Bob Woodward and Carl Bernstein, writing in the *Washington Post*, allege that the Watergate break-in was part of a larger campaign of political espionage and "dirty tricks." In their reporting, they rely on an anonymous source who comes to be called "Deep Throat."

November 7: Nixon and his vice president, Spiro Agnew, are reelected in a landslide victory with 61 percent of the popular vote.

December 8: Dorothy Hunt (Howard Hunt's wife) is killed in a plane crash. Her purse is found, stuffed with $100 bills.

1973

January 8: The Watergate trial of Liddy, Hunt, McCord, and the burglars begins.

January 11: Senator Sam Ervin (D-NC) agrees to lead the Senate investigation of Watergate.

January 23: Nixon announces that U.S. combat troops will leave Vietnam on January 28, ending U.S. involvement in the war.

February 7: The Senate Select Committee on Presidential Campaign

Activities (the Ervin Committee) is officially established.

March 19: McCord writes a letter to Judge John J. Sirica saying that there's been a cover-up and that people have been lying to the court.

March 21: Nixon's devices record Dean's warning to the president that there is a "cancer . . . close to the presidency."

April 16: Dean meets with Nixon for the last time and suspects that he might be being taped.

April 30: Nixon announces the resignations of his top aides John Ehrlichman and Haldeman and the firing of Dean.

May 7: The new attorney general, Elliot Richardson, says that he will appoint a special prosecutor with broad powers to resolve the Watergate scandal.

May 11: Charges against Ellsberg are dismissed when it is revealed that the Watergate burglars had previously broken into his psychiatrist's office.

May 17: The televised Watergate hearings begin.

May 18: Archibald Cox is appointed special prosecutor.

June 25: Dean testifies at the Watergate hearings.

July 16: Alexander Butterfield testifies that Nixon's office had secret taping devices.

July 23: Cox gets the grand jury to subpoena Nixon's tapes.

August 29: Sirica orders the White House to turn over the tapes.

October 10: Vice President Agnew pleads no contest to a charge of income tax evasion and resigns.

October 12: Nixon appoints House minority leader Gerald Ford as vice president.

October 19: Dean pleads guilty.

October 20: Cox holds a press conference to say that he will demand that Nixon release relevant Oval Office tapes. Nixon refuses. Nixon orders the attorney general to fire Cox. He refuses, as does the deputy attorney general. Nixon fires both of them. Robert Bork, the solicitor general, agrees to fire Cox. (This sequence of actions became known as the Saturday Night Massacre.)

October 23: The House announces the beginning of an impeachment inquiry.

November 1: Cox's replacement as special prosecutor, Leon Jaworski, is appointed.

November 21: The Ervin

Committee announces that there is an eighteen-and-a-half-minute gap in the crucial June 20, 1972, tape.

November 26: Nixon's secretary, Rose Mary Woods, testifies on the gap, trying to demonstrate how it happened. (Her pose is called the "Rose Mary Stretch.")

1974

February 6: The House of Representatives votes 410 to 4 to proceed with an impeachment investigation.

May 9: The House Judiciary Committee begins formal hearings on the impeachment of President Nixon.

July 24: The Supreme Court rules that President Nixon has no right to withhold any of the White House tapes. Nixon agrees.

July 27: By a vote of 27 to 11, the House Judiciary Committee recommends that Nixon be impeached.

August 5: Nixon releases an edited version of the tapes to the public. (Members of Congress and the public do not feel that this is acceptable.)

August 8: Nixon announces on television that he will resign.

August 9: At noon, Nixon resigns and Ford is sworn in as president.

September 8: Ford grants a full and unconditional pardon to Nixon.

September 28: The Ervin Committee submits its final report.

AFTERMATH

1977: Nixon gives his first major interview about Watergate, telling TV journalist David Frost: "Well, when the president does it, that means that it is not illegal."

1994: Nixon dies and is buried with full honors.

2005: FBI agent Mark Felt, now ninety-one years old, admits that he is Deep Throat. Woodward and Bernstein confirm this.

NOTE ON SOURCES

In this book, we have made use of many public documents, excerpts from the Nixon Tapes, speeches, Senate hearings, etc. The material is vast. Some of the Nixon Tapes have not even been transcribed, and others that have been transcribed have not been indexed. For the quotes we used in our book, we have provided citations but not necessarily URLs. The documents are available in a wide variety of locations. You'll also see the abbreviation *ibid.* a lot in the sources. Ibid. is short for *ibidem*, which, in Latin, means "in the same place." In the source notes, ibid. means the quote it's referring to is from the same source as the quote directly above it.

Students who are using this book as a way to research Watergate and the presidency of Richard Nixon will find that our citations lead them to the major repositories of archival material. Some are easier to navigate than others. We found the Richard Nixon Presidential Library and Museum and the Miller Center for Presidential Studies at the University of Virginia easier to use than the National Archives and congressional records. We want our readers to understand that there are many ways to locate information.

Another important point is that while each quotation may be accurate, the speaker might not have told the truth. But those contradictions are why your authors love history.

SOURCE NOTES

INTRODUCTION

vi "When the President does it . . .": David Frost, television interview with Richard Nixon, May 19, 1977.

xiii "It is very different today": Mary McCarthy, *The Mask of State: Watergate Portraits* (New York: Harcourt Brace Jovanovich, 1974), 55.

TO BE A FLY ON THE WALL

2 "He'd never be able": John Ehrlichman, *Witness to Power: The Nixon Years* (New York: Simon & Schuster, 1982), 82.

3 "Mum's the word": Nixon Tapes, February 16, 1971, Nixon Library, Conversation 450-10, 10:28 a.m. Douglas Brinkley et al., page 5, nixonlibrary.gov/forresearchers/find/tapes/finding _aids/tapesubjectlogs/oval450.pdf.

4 "Nixon and I agreed": H. R. Haldeman, "The Nixon White House Tapes: The Decision to Record Presidential Conversations," *Prologue Magazine* 30, no. 2 (Summer 1988).

5 "Mr. President, you'll never remember": Ibid.

5 "We knew he'd never be able": Ehrlichman, *Witness to Power*, 82.

THE GANG THAT COULDN'T BURGLE STRAIGHT

6 "I don't think I had ever seen": Karlyn Barker and Walter Pincus, "Watergate Revisited: Twenty Years After the Break-In," *Washington Post*, June 14, 1992.

7 "Your rental time is up": Rick Perlstein, *Nixonland: The Rise of a President and the Fracturing of America* (New York: Scribner, 2008), 666.

7–8 "Gordon, I know you like . . . 'I'd swear it was piss'": G. Gordon Liddy, *Will: The Autobiography of G. Gordon Liddy* (New York: St. Martin's Press, 1980), 230–31.

9 "There's a burglary": Barker and Pincus, "Watergate Revisited."

9 "We didn't jump out": Ibid.

9–10 "Hey, any of our guys . . . all this electrical stuff": Liddy, *Will*, 218.

10 "Officer Barrett eyed one man": Barker and Pincus, "Watergate Revisited."

10 "I found penlights": Ibid.

11 "I said, 'Wait a minute,'": Ibid.

11 "We began packing everything . . . be going to jail": Liddy, *Will*, 221.

12 "They should not be released": Earl J. Silbert, "Present Status of Watergate Investigation Conducted by the United States Attorney for the District of Columbia," June 7, 1973, National Archives.

12–13 "What are your professions . . . CIA": Alfred Lewis, "Five Held in Plot to Bug Democrats' Office Here," *Washington Post*, June 18, 1972.

13 "Holy sh*t": Carl Bernstein and Bob Woodward, *All the President's Men* (40th anniversary ed., New York: Simon & Schuster, 2014), 18.

14 "I dismissed it as some": Richard Nixon, *RN: The Memoirs of Richard Nixon* (New York: Touchstone, 1978), 626.

14 "Of all the sordid Watergate cast": "Watergate: The Tough Guy," *Time*, September 24, 1973.

14 "WHEN YOU'VE GOT THEM": Charles Colson, *Born Again: What Really Happened to the White House Hatchet Man* (Old Tappan, NJ: Chosen Books, 1976), 16.

15 "This is not one that . . . They certainly do": Ibid., 21.

THE PLUMBERS

16 "Since my will was now": Liddy, *Will*, 129.

16 "I am much inflamed": George Washington, "George Washington to Officers of the Army," March 15, 1783, National Archives.

17 "Every President needs a": Evan Thomas, *Being Nixon: A Man Divided* (New York: Random House, 2015), 198–99.

17 "Well, when the president does it": David Frost, television interview with Richard Nixon, May 19, 1977.

18 "I was talking to my mother-in-law": Fred Emery, *Watergate: The Corruption of American Politics and the Fall of Richard Nixon* (New York: Touchstone, 1994), 57.

18–19 "Since my will was now . . . a Swiss airplane pilot": Liddy, *Will*, 119–20.

19 "I have found my": Thomas, *Being Nixon*, 153.

20 "Nixon couldn't piss straight": Ibid.

20 "From the beginning she was the darling": Madeleine Edmondson and Alden Duer Cohen, *The Women of Watergate* (New York: Stein & Day, 1975), 38–41.

20 "I love to wind my tongue": Ibid., 44.

21 "Quitting the Justice Department": Vivian Cadden, "Martha Mitchell: The Day the Laughing Stopped," *McCall's Magazine*, July 1973.

21 "We had a meeting with": Liddy, *Will*, 196.

21 "[We can] identify the leaders": Ibid., 273.

22 "Gordon, a million dollars . . . Yes, sir": Ibid., 196–98.

23 "Gordon, do you think you can . . . photograph whatever you find": Ibid., 138.

23 "Although I was aware": Jeb Stuart Magruder, *An American Life: One Man's Road to Watergate* (New York, Atheneum, 1974), 219.

A SMOKING GUN

24 "It's a third-rate burglary attempt": Ron Ziegler, June 18, 1972, Miller Center, University of Virginia.

24 "We were pleased that the": Liddy, *Will*, 349.

24–25 "It's fortunately a bizarre story . . . to be like Nathan Hale": Nixon Tapes, June 20, 1972.

26 "Now, on the investigation . . . we are going to play it": Nixon Tapes, June 23, 1972.

26 "The basic goal of the cover story": Magruder, *An American Life*, 228–31.

INSIDE NIXON'S HEAD

27 "[My father] had a lemon ranch": "Nixon's Farewell Address, White House," August 9, 1974, Public Papers of Richard Nixon.

28 "He was very fussy": Thomas, *Being Nixon*, 7.

28 "Can you imagine what this man": Hugh Sidey, "The Presidency: Interview with Henry Kissinger," *Time*, August 28, 1978.

28 "The hour on stage was agony": Nixon, *RN*, 14.

29 "Oh how I hate Richard Nixon": Thomas, *Being Nixon*, 5.

29 "[My friends asked me] how I could abide": Ibid., 16.

30 "They [the Franklins] were the haves": Ibid., 13.

30 "We used him as a punching bag": Ibid., 13.

30 "I always thought": Ibid., 17.

30–31 "I knew these firms hired": Ibid., 23.

31 "I could not take my eyes": Nixon, *RN*, 21.

31 "I am certainly not the Romeo type": Will Smith, "Richard Nixon, Hopeless Romantic," *Politico*, February 13, 2014.

32 "People reach to fear": William Safire, *Before the Fall: An Insider View of the Pre-Watergate White House* (New York: Doubleday, 1975), 9.

32–33 "I should say this . . . we are going to keep it": Richard Nixon, Checkers speech, September 23, 1952.

33 "No man except Franklin D. Roosevelt": Theodore White, *Breach of Faith: The Fall of Richard Nixon* (New York, Atheneum, 1975), 66.

34 "I told my staff": Nixon, *RN*, 474.

34 "[That] . . . the coming election year": Liddy, *Will*, 179.

STRUGGLE AT HOME AND WAR IN VIETNAM

35 "It is difficult now to describe": Ron Elving, "George McGovern: An Improbable Icon of Anti-War Movement," NPR.org, October 22, 2012.

36 "Why should they ask me": Bob Orkand, "'I Ain't Got No Quarrel with Them Vietcong,'" *New York Times*, June 27, 2017.

37 "I work my ass off": Pete Hamill, "The Revolt of the White Lower Middle Class," *New York*, April 14, 1969.

39 "We see Americans hating each other": Richard Nixon, acceptance speech, Republican National Convention, August 8, 1968.

39 "I am not going to be the first": National Archives, "Remembering Vietnam: Online Exhibit," Episode 9: Crossing into Cambodia, n.d.

40 "This is treasonable action": Nixon Tapes, June 15, 1971.

40 "This has been for me . . . help end this war?": Steve Sheinkin, *Most Dangerous: Daniel Ellsberg and the Secret History of the Vietnam War* (New York: Roaring Brook Press, 2015), 249.

41 "What did [you] find . . . in search of drugs": Ibid., 250.

41 "[Magruder testified that] he began": "The Short of It" (editorial), *North Adams Transcript*, June 16, 1973.

42 "The bastards have never": Daniel Ellsberg, *Secrets: A Memoir of Vietnam and the Pentagon Papers* (New York: Penguin, 2003), 426.

42 "Tonight, I want to talk to you": Richard Nixon, "Vietnamization" speech, November 3, 1969.

BLACKMAIL

44 "We won't leave . . .": John W. Dean, *Blind Ambition: The White House Years* (New York: Simon & Schuster, 1976), 116.

45 "The only way to get rid": Liddy, *Will*, 359.

45 "Sure enough, there were thirteen": Ibid., 359.

46 "Bring money and the name . . . five days after Watergate": Ibid., 362.

47 "I called Dean, who had just returned": Magruder, *An American Life*, 223–24.

47 "It was obvious that Dean": Liddy, *Will*, 352.

47 "Gordon, I think we ought to . . . and so forth": John Dean, *Blind Ambition*, 114.

47–48 "I see. Gordon, I think . . . I don't think we're really there": Ibid., 98.

48–49 "Three workmen in green . . . won't leave any prints": Ibid., 116.

49 "We found a revolver": Ibid., 114, 115.

50 "Ehrlichman suggested I": Ibid., 121–22.

50 "These should never see": L. Patrick Gray III, with Ed Gray and Michael Prichard, *In Nixon's Web: A Year in the Crosshairs of Watergate* (New York: Times Books, 2010), 81–82.

50 "I made the gravest mistake": Richard A. Serrano, "L. Patrick Gray, 88; Led FBI Under Nixon," *Los Angeles Times*, June 7, 2005.

51 "It was an overcrowded": Emery, *Watergate*, 152.

51–52 "Meet me in Lafayette Park . . . quickly adjourned the meeting": John Dean, *Blind Ambition*, 123.

52–53 "On June 28, I received . . . get rid of it was a problem": Tony Ulasewicz, with Stuart A. McKeever, *The President's Private Eye: The Journey of Detective Tony U. from N.Y.P.D. to the Nixon White House* (Westport, CT: MASCAM Publishing, 1990), 250.

UNDER THE BUS: PART I

54 "We would leak out the fact": Nixon Tapes, July 28, 1972.

54 "As soon as they called it": *All the President's Men Revisited*, MSNBC, June 17, 2013.

55 "I'm sick and tired": Vivian Cadden, "Martha Mitchell: The Day the Laughing Stopped," *McCall's*, July 1973.

55 "I am a political prisoner": Helen Thomas, "Martha Is 'Leaving' Mitchell," *Washington Post*, June 26, 1972.

56 "Maybe we should send her . . . she aware of Watergate?": Nixon Tapes, June 29, 1972.

57 "Being the wife of a politician . . . she always will, but . . .": Nixon Tapes, June 30, 1972.

58 "If it hadn't been for Martha": David Frost, "Nixon Interview: Watergate, Part 1," May 5, 1977.

58–59 "We would leak out the fact . . . [welfare of my wife and daughter] . . .": Stanley Kutler, *Abuse of Power: The New Nixon Tapes* (New York: Free Press, 1997).

FOUR MORE YEARS!

60 "After so many rebuffs": Maureen Dean, with Hays Gorey, *"Mo": A Woman's View of Watergate* (New York: Simon & Schuster, 1975), 101.

61 "The best way to assure": H. R. Haldeman, *The Haldeman Diaries* (New York: G. P. Putnam's Sons, 1994), entry for April 29, 1972.

61 "McGovern is speaking": Thomas, *Being Nixon*, 399.

61–62 "[Eagleton] had been in the hospital . . . against overwhelming odds": Ibid., 400.

62 "Do you know what my": Ibid., 400.

64 "My eyes burned from the": Nixon, *RN*, 174.

64 "He's obviously enjoying this": Hunter S. Thompson, *The Great Shark Hunt: Strange Tales from a Strange Time* (New York: Summit Books, 1979), 186.

64 About seventy of every hundred: Gladys Engel Lang and Kurt Lang, *The Battle for Public Opinion: The President, the Press, and the Polls During Watergate* (New York: Columbia University Press, 1983), 28.

THE STORY THAT FADES BUT DOESN'T GO AWAY

65 "We had persuaded ourselves": Magruder, *An American Life*, 103.

65–66 "This is about bugging": McGovern Watergate ad, 1972, posted by ElectionWallDotOrg, YouTube, youtube.com/watch?v=BTazql0sw9o.

66 "Senator George McGovern now appears": *St. Louis Globe-Democrat*, August 17, 1972.

66 "We told other reporters": Magruder, *An American Life*, 103.

67 "The managing editor of ": Bernstein and Woodward, *All the President's Men*, 71.

67 "We would meet [at]": Bob Woodward, "How Mark Felt Became 'Deep Throat,'" *Washington Post*, June 20, 2005.

68 "When [Woodward and Bernstein] uncovered": John Dean, *Blind Ambition*, 71.

68 "We had persuaded ourselves": Magruder, *An American Life*, 103.

69 "All the testimony you are about to give": Brendan Koerner, "Where Did We Get Our

Oath?" *Slate*, n.d., slate.com/articles/news_and_politics/explainer/2004/04/where_did _we_get_our_oath.html.

69 "I had been ordered . . . might have to": John Dean, *The Nixon Defense: What He Knew and When He Knew It* (New York: Viking, 2014), 103.

69–70 "[Sloan] and his wife . . . easy to lose perspective": Bernstein and Woodward, *All the President's Men*, 84.

70 "[We] began almost by instinct": James M. Naughton, "Magruder on Watergate: Ends Justify the Means," *New York Times*, June 15, 1973.

71 "Mr. President, wouldn't it be . . . very bizarre incident": John Dean, *Blind Ambition*, 136.

71 "I damn near fell off . . . nasty problem like Watergate": Ibid., 137.

71–72 "I knew something the public": Maureen Dean, *"Mo,"* 61.

72 "There was never any consideration": Naughton, "Magruder on Watergate."

72 "John Mitchell, while serving": Carl Bernstein and Bob Woodward, "Mitchell Controlled Secret GOP Fund," *Washington Post*, September 29, 1972.

72–73 "Sir, I am sorry to bother you . . . most sickening thing I've ever heard": Bernstein and Woodward, *All the President's Men*, 104.

73–74 "Did Mitchell definitely understand . . . desk I said it was okay": Ibid., 105.

ENEMIES, ENEMIES, EVERYWHERE

75 "Somewhere in the 1972 campaign": Jimmy Breslin, *How the Good Guys Finally Won: Notes from an Impeachment Summer* (New York: Viking Press, 1975), 124.

76 "I did something I rarely did": Magruder, *An American Life*, 252.

76 "As might be expected, federal": *News and Courier*, September 19, 1972.

76 "It's whitewash . . .": Douglas E. Kneeland, "McGovern Accuses Nixon of Whitewash on Break-In," *New York Times*, September 17, 1972.

76–77 "Well, you had quite a day . . . That's an exciting prospect": John Dean, *Blind Ambition*, 135–39.

77 "This is a war . . . tried to do us in": Nixon Tapes, September 15, 1972.

78 "Never forget: The press": Nixon Tapes, December 14, 1972.

78 "This memorandum addresses the matter": "Transcript of White House Memo on Dean's Senate Testimony and His Comments," *New York Times*, June 28, 1973.

78–79 "It's like a heavyweight fight": Nixon Tapes, August 3, 1972.

79 "Geez, Tip, I want to tell you . . . concentrating on the shakedown": Breslin, *How the Good Guys Finally Won*, viii.

A BIG WIN, BUT NOBODY'S HAPPY

80 "I am at a loss to explain": Nixon, *RN*, 715.

81 "Stop it!": Rowland Evans and Robert Novack, *Nixon in the White House* (New York: Random House, 1971), 413.

81 "Election night was anti-climactic": Magruder, *An American Life*, 225.

82 "I am at a loss to explain": Nixon, *RN*, 715.

82 "It was sort of grim": Thomas, *Being Nixon*, 441.

82 "The entire senior staff . . . you about the specifics": John Dean, *Blind Ambition*, 206.

82 "I stood up and in chilling tones": Haldeman, *The Haldeman Diaries*, 224.

83 "I see this now as a mistake": Nixon, *RN*, 769.

BLACK CLOUDS: WITHOUT A SILVER LINING

86 "I'll show them I know how to die": Liddy, *Will*, 380–81.

87 "I don't think we should sit": "Judge Urges Further Probe of Bugging," *Louisville Courier-Journal*, February 3, 1973, 6.

87–88 "She acted like a gambling": Quoted in St. John Hunt, *Dorothy, "An Amoral and Dangerous Woman": The Murder of E. Howard Hunt's Wife—Watergate's Darkest Secret* (Walterville, OR: Trine Day, 2014), 88.

88 "Commitments were made . . . action for Christ's sake": Emery, *Watergate*, 226–27.

88–89 "After what happened . . . should have clemency": Nixon, *RN*, 745.

89 "Gordon, I want to assure you . . . know how to die": Liddy, *Will*, 380–81.

90 "The jury is going to want": Walter Rugaber, "Watergate Trial: Judge Indicates Political Aspects of the Case Will Be Examined," *New York Times*, December 5, 1972.

91 "[Howard Hunt arrived] wearing": Walter Rugaber, "Watergate Trial Opens; Jury Screening Begins," *New York Times*, January 8, 1973.

91 "I don't think we should . . . I don't believe you": "Judge Urges Further Probe of Bugging."

91–92 "Furthermore, Defendant Barker had no way": *Boston Globe*, February 1, 1973.

92 "I would frankly hope": Judge John J. Sirica, statement at bail hearing, February 2, 1973, as quoted in Samuel Dash, *Chief Counsel: Inside the Ervin Committee—The Untold Story of Watergate* (New York: Random House, 1976), 5.

92 "Here's the judge saying": Nixon Tapes, February 3, 1973.

FUZZY EYEBROWS

93 "I'm just an old": Sam J. Ervin Jr., *Humor of a Country Lawyer* (Chapel Hill: University of North Carolina Press, 1984), 23.

93 "Our senators are nothing": Nixon Tapes, February 3, 1973.

94 "We won the election": Creation of the Senate Select Committee on Presidential Campaign Activities, Committee Papers, National Archives No. 12171890, February 7, 1973.

94 "To investigate violations of the election laws": Ibid.

94 "I'm just an old": Ervin, *Humor of a Country Lawyer*, 23.

95 "The United States Constitution": "Ervin, A Tough Man to Label," *Abilene Reporter-News*, January 1, 1971, 50.

95 "The Watergate investigation is a mighty": Dash, *Chief Counsel*, 6.

95 "Watergate is starting to snowball": Nixon, *RN*, 770.

96 "I'm not going to let anybody": Nixon Tapes, February 28, 1973.

NAMING NAMES

97 "The jail was 104 years old": Liddy, *Will*, 397.

97 Gordon Liddy tried to impress: Ibid., 405.

98 "McCord actually believed": Ibid., 399.

98 "In the interests of justice": *United States v. George Gordon Liddy et. al.*, C.R. 1827–72, United States District Court for the District of Columbia; Records of District Courts of the United States, Record Group 21; NARA, College Park, MD.

98–99 "Perjury occurred during the trial . . . that it was not": Ibid.

99–100 "You must understand": Ibid.

100 "When I returned to my office": Dash, *Chief Counsel*, 31.

100 "I was impressed with McCord's sincerity": Emery, *Watergate*, 274.

A CANCER ON THE PRESIDENCY

101 "We could get a million dollars": Nixon Tapes, March 21, 1973.

101 "He told me things were": Maureen Dean, *"Mo,"* 191.

102–03 "We have a cancer . . . sort of the basic facts": Nixon Tapes, March 21, 1973.

103 "How much money do you . . . dealing in that business": Ibid.

103–04 "After he told President Nixon": Maureen Dean, *"Mo,"* 200.

104 "Don't, don't go into . . . like a blanket": Nixon Tapes, March 21, 1973.

104 "John Dean III, my beloved": Maureen Dean, *"Mo,"* 203.

UNDER THE BUS: PART II

105 "John had to look after": Ibid., 163.

105 "John, you're in big trouble . . . be more encouraging": John Dean, *Blind Ambition*, 227.

106 "John Dean told me a fantastic story": Dash, *Chief Counsel*, 92.

106 "[Nixon] seemed exhausted": John Dean, *The Nixon Defense*, 213.

107 "Mr. President, what you have to realize . . . you as a president": Thomas, *Being Nixon*, 444.

107–08 "The P[resident] was in . . . wake up this morning": Haldeman, *The Haldeman Diaries*, entry for April 29, 1973.

108 "Your turn . . . About as expected": Ibid.

108–09 "It's like cutting off . . . used on both of us": Ibid.

109–10 "There can be no whitewash . . . my privilege to know": Richard Nixon, "Address to the Nation," July 31, 1973.

110 "The Counsel to the President . . . never, never, never": Nixon Tapes, April 30, 1973.

IMPEACHMENT ON THE HORIZON

111 "The Watergate whirlpool is swirling": Edward W. Knappman, ed., *Watergate and the White House*, Vol. 1 (New York: Facts on File, 1973), 183.

111–12 "The resignation of three": Ibid., 174.

112 "The Watergate dam burst": Ibid., 179.

112 "These Watergate scoundrels are the very persons": Ibid., 179.

113–14 "Speculation about impeachment of President Nixon": *Worcester Telegram*, May 6, 1973.

114 "The time is going to come": Breslin, *How the Good Guys Finally Won*, 15.

114 "We are appalled by the sewer of hatred": *Burlington Free Press*, May 15, 1973.

ARCHIBALD COX TO THE RESCUE

115 "[Archibald Cox was a] partisan viper": Nixon, *RN*, 929.

115–16 "I wish I could say": Sheinkin, *Most Dangerous*, 305.

116 "On and on come the ugly revelations": *Congressional Record*, May 9, 1973, 15085.

116 "He's sort of Mr. Integrity": Nixon Tapes, April 29, 1973.

116 "I have given him absolute authority": Richard Nixon, speech to the public, April 30, 1973.

117 "Elliot, the one thing . . . I'll think about it, sir": Nixon Tapes, April 30, 1973.

117 "[Cox had] an unmistakable": J. Anthony Lukas, *Nightmare: The Underside of the Nixon Years* (New York: Viking, 1976), 418.

117–18 "Even though that trail . . . decency of government": Nomination of Elliot Richardson to Attorney General, Hearing, Committee of Judiciary, U.S. Senate, May 21, 1973.

118 "If [Elliot Richardson] had searched": Nixon, *RN*, 929.

EVERYBODY'S WATCHING

119 "On May 17, 1973, 11 months after": Lang and Lang, *The Battle for Public Opinion*, 62.

119–20 "The Founding Fathers knew . . . in their own elections": Senate Select Committee on Presidential Campaign Activities, May 17, 1973.

120 "By the second week of hearings": Lang and Lang, *The Battle for Public Opinion*, 62.

121 "They don't realize what": Nixon Tapes, June 13, 1973.

121 "You need a strong man": "True Believers," *Slate* podcast, January 1, 2018.

122 "The White House was betting": John Dean, *Blind Ambition*, 304.

122 "Much of the nation sat": Maureen Dean, "*Mo*," 253.

122–23 "I relied on my own fashion instinct . . . not to everyone, but to many": Ibid., 262.

123–24 "I have in my possession . . . happy to submit them": Senate Select Committee on Presidential Campaign Activities, June 27, 1973.

124 "Number 17, Daniel Schorr": Quoted in Jordy Yager, "Journalist Recalls the Honor of Being on Nixon's Enemies List," *The Hill*, January 6, 2009.

124 "I have had a mixed reaction": Tom Wicker, "Enemies of the People," *New York Times*, June 29, 1973.

124 "The action of the plumbers": Senate Select Committee on Presidential Campaign Activities, July 18, 1973.

125 "There is a famous principle of law . . . pretty legitimate principle of law": Ibid., July 16, 1973.

125 "It's unbelievable that something like this": Steven V. Roberts, "Public Found Disillusioned by the Watergate Scandal," *New York Times*, August 13, 1973.

TAPES, TAPES, WHO'S GOT THE TAPES?

126 "Mr. Nixon has tried mightily to portray": "Privilege, Precedent and Mr. Dean" (editorial), *Washington Post*, March 26, 1973.

126 "What did the president know": Emery, *Watergate*, 362.

127 "Did you hear about the new": Roy Reed, "Watergate Comics Find the Joke Is on Them," *New York Times*, September 8, 1973.

127–28 "I wanted to feel that . . . and he steals": "Privilege, Precedent and Mr. Dean."

129 "What makes you think . . . just as I know it": "Privilege, Precedent and Mr. Dean."

129–30 "John, let me ask you this . . . Alexander Butterfield": John Dean, *Blind Ambition*, 331.

130 "Mr. Butterfield, are you aware . . . yes, sir": Senate Select Committee on Presidential Campaign Activities, July 16, 1973.

130 "The tape recordings": James M. Naughton, "Surprise Witness: Butterfield, Ex-Aide at White House, Tells of Listening Devices," *New York Times*, July 17, 1973.

131 "Boss, you've got to": Thomas, *Being Nixon*, 480.

131 "If the president broke the confidence": Nixon, "Address to the Nation," July 31, 1973.

132 "No writ of executive privilege": Senate Select Committee on Presidential Campaign Activities, July 23, 1973.

132 "Well, when the president does it": David Frost, television interview with Richard Nixon, May 19, 1977.

THE LAW VERSUS RICHARD NIXON

133 "If we have a confrontation": House Judiciary Impeachment Hearings, Richardson Affidavit.

133–34 "Order that respondent": Grand Jury Subpoena *Duces Tecum* issued to Richard M. Nixon, United States District Court of District of Columbia, August 19, 1973.

134 "With the utmost respect for the court": Richard Nixon, "Letter Responding to a District Court Subpoena Requiring Production of Presidential Tape Recordings and Documents," July 26, 1973, presidency.ucsb.edu/node/255705.

134 "The impending clash threatens": *Watergate and the White House*, Vol. 1, 153.

134 "I will not tear down": Richard Nixon, Brief to the United States Court of Appeals, September 19, 1973.

134 "I have a four-year-old who watches": *Watergate and the White House*, Vol. 1, 146.

135 "The hearings are very political . . . our capacity to understand": Ibid.

135 "Our adversaries . . . wish to": Lukas, *Nightmare*, 420.

136–37 "In the 1960s": Richard Nixon, "Address to the Nation on Watergate," August 15, 1973.

137 "The people want the facts": Lang and Lang, *The Battle for Public Opinion*, 82.

137 "Why doesn't the President resign": Richard Nixon, "Speech to Executive Club," Chicago, March 15, 1974.

137 "At some point in the hot muggy summer": Nixon, *RN*, 961.

138 "Can you imagine Gerry Ford": Emery, *Watergate*, 384.

138 "Though the President is elected": United States Circuit Court of Appeals, October 12, 1973.

SATURDAY NIGHT MASSACRE

140 "Whether we shall continue": Quoted in Tim Weiner, *One Man Against the World: The Tragedy of Richard Nixon* (New York: Henry Holt, 2015), 267.

140 "She would die for him": Lukas, *Nightmare*, 461.

141–42 "I might have caused . . . I agreed to at all": Dash, *Chief Counsel*, 211.

142 "I cannot be a party . . . Hell no": Lukas, *Nightmare*, 435.

142 "More than ever, I wanted": Nixon, *RN*, 931.

142 "Nixon believed that he had absolute": Dash, *Chief Counsel*, 186.

143 "All day, newsmen in unusual numbers": Douglas E. Kneeland, "Nixon Discharges Cox for Defiance; Abolishes Watergate Task Force; Richardson and Ruckelshaus Out," *New York Times*, October 21, 1973.

143 "I am certainly not out to get": Emery, *Watergate*, 396–97.

143 "On orders from your Commander . . . I'd better come over to resign": Lukas, *Nightmare*, 437.

144 "Mr. President, I feel . . . Fire Cox": Ibid.

144 "Discharge Cox immediately": Carroll Kilpatrick, "Nixon Forces Firing of Cox; Richardson, Ruckelshaus Quit," *Washington Post*, October 21, 1973.

145 "The President has discharged Cox": Ibid.

145 "The country tonight is in the midst": Thomas, *Being Nixon*, 473.

145 "We all expected something to happen": Leslie Oelsner, "Cox Office Shut on Nixon's Orders," *New York Times*, October 21, 1973.

146 "If Haig had deliberately tried": Emery, *Watergate*, 401.

146 "By late [that] evening": Kneeland, "Nixon Discharges Cox."

146 "Richard Nixon and the nation": Henry Grunwald, "The President Should Resign" (editorial), *Time*, November 12, 1973.

TEETERING ON THE EDGE

147 "People have got to know": Richard Nixon, press conference, November 17, 1973.

147 "It is a grave time in American history" (editorial), *Atlanta Constitution*, October 22, 1973.

148 Immediately after what became known: Amy B. Wang, "The Saturday Night Massacre: 'Your Commander in Chief Has Given You an Order,'" *Washington Post*, May 11, 2017.

148 "In a statement, . . . the Congressional Black Caucus": James M. Naughton, "Democrats Firm: House Panel Will Move 'Full Steam Ahead,' Chairman Says," *New York Times*, October 25, 1973.

148 "[Rodino] exhibited a great": Breslin, *How the Good Guys Finally Won*, 180.

148–49 "When Congress reconvened": Emery, *Watergate*, 404.

149 "The President of the United States . . . does not defy the law": John J. Sirica, *To Set the Record Straight: The Break-In, the Tapes, the Conspirators, the Pardon* (New York: Norton, 1979), 175–79.

149 "It was a new phase in": Lukas, *Nightmare*, 443.

150 "Rodino said . . . [We will] proceed full steam ahead": Naughton, "Democrats Firm," *New York Times*, October 25, 1973.

150 "I have never heard or seen . . . angry with those he respects": Richard Nixon, press conference, October 26, 1973.

151 "The startling revelation": Lukas, *Nightmare*, 489.

151 "People have got to know": Richard Nixon, press conference, November 17, 1973.

151 "I was only ten years old": *All the President's Men Revisited*, MSNBC, June 17, 2013.

152 "Are we going to be blindsided": Lang and Lang, *The Battle for Public Opinion*, 120.

152 "President Nixon's personal secretary": R. W. Apple Jr., "Nixon Secretary Linked to Erasure," *New York Times*, November 26, 1973.

153 "[The gap in the tape]": John J. Sirica, courtroom hearing, November 20, 1974.

154 "I think the alternatives": "Charles Mathias, Former US Senator, Dies at 87," *New York Times*, January 25, 2019.

LULL BEFORE THE SUPREME STORM

155 "There is a time to fly": Lukas, *Nightmare*, 476.

155 "My father was more tense and uncommunicative": John Farrell, *Richard Nixon: The Life* (New York: Doubleday, 2017), 511.

156 "The White House Christmas party": Colson, *Born Again*, 197.

157 "Do I fight all out": Nixon, *RN*, 971.

157 "The biggest danger I saw in the year ahead": Ibid., 544.

157 "Just be damned sure . . . how to commit perjury?": James Doyle, *Not Above the Law: The Battle of Watergate Prosecutors Cox and Jaworski* (New York: Morrow, 1977), 265.

158 "The mere fact of an impeachment inquiry": R. W. Apple Jr., "Nixon Is Unwilling to Yield More Tapes to House Unit," *New York Times*, March 13, 1974.

158 "You know how he talks": Thomas, *Being Nixon*, 460.

159 "This president has nothing to hide": Richard Nixon, "Address to the Nation Announcing Answer to the House Judiciary Committee Subpoena for Additional Presidential Tape Recordings," April 29, 1974.

160 "I felt like throwing up": Farrell, *Richard Nixon*, 526.

160 "The White House gambit": Doyle, *Not Above the Law*, 267.

161 "We did not subpoena an edited": Lukas, *Nightmare*, 493.

DYING BY INCHES

162 "We are dying by inches": Farrell, *Richard Nixon*, 525.

162–63 "We think the end is near": *Miami Herald*, August 7, 1974.

163 "He took out a pad of paper": Farrell, *Richard Nixon*, 525.

163–65 "Our judgment is not concerned . . . a twentieth-century paper shredder": *Watergate and the White House*, Vol. 3, 248.

165 "Anyone watching the televised operations": (editorial), *Manchester Union Leader*, July 30, 1974.

165 "Lowest point in the presidency": Nixon, *RN*, 1050.

166 "Inside this building, with its marble hallways": Elizabeth Drew, *Washington Journal: The Events of 1973–1976* (New York: Vintage, 1976), 304.

166–67 "What public interest is there . . . immune in all circumstances": *United States v. Richard Nixon*, U.S. Supreme Court, July 24, 1974.

167 "The President considered defying the high court": Doyle, *Not Above the Law*, 267.

167 "That was how I learned that I was": Nixon, *RN*, 1051.

BACK TO CALIFORNIA

168 "To leave office before my term is completed": Richard Nixon, "Address Announcing Resignation," August 8, 1974.

169 "When the smoking gun was released": John Dean, *The Nixon Defense*, 646.

169 "In a sharp setback to his fight": John Herbers, "Tapes Released," *New York Times*, August 6, 1974.

169 "Any delay now is only a question": McClory, *Congressional Quarterly*, August 5, 1974.

170 "The President was up walking the halls": Bob Woodward and Carl Bernstein, *The Final Days* (New York: Simon & Schuster, 1976), 395.

171 "If the president gave any nuclear launch order": Garrett M. Graff, "The Madman and the Bomb," *Politico*, August 11, 2017.

171 "Dear Daddy. I love you": Farrell, *Richard Nixon*, 530.

172 "We told him the situation": Woodward and Bernstein, *The Final Days*, 416.

172–73 "Mr. President, this isn't pleasant . . . There'll be no tears": Ibid.

173 "The official White House position": John Herbers, "'Gloomy' Picture," *New York Times*, August 8, 1974.

173 "We're going back to California . . . and there we are smiling": Woodward and Bernstein, *The Final Days*, 421.

174 "I went to . . . starting to settle in": Nixon, *RN*, 974.

174 "At 12:30 this afternoon": Philip Shabecoff, "Only Nixon Is Serene at Sad White House," *New York Times*, August 9, 1974.

174 "Yesterday I saw a degree of anguish": Ibid.

174–75 "Outside the White House . . . gonna see too much in a lifetime": Lukas, *Nightmare*, 561.

175 "I've got a little bit of a cold . . . Is that true or not?": "Nixon Resignation," Clip from "President Nixon's Resignation Address," August 8, 1974, C-SPAN, May 7, 2015, c-span .org/video/?c4536919/nixon-resignation.

175–76 "Good evening, this is the thirty-seventh time": Nixon, "Address Announcing Resignation," August 8, 1974.

176–77 "We think that when someone": Richard Nixon, "Farewell Address in the White House," August 9, 1974.

177 "My fellow Americans": "Gerald R. Ford's Remarks Upon Taking the Oath of Office as President," Gerald R. Ford Presidential Library and Museum, fordlibrarymuseum.gov /library/speeches/740001.asp.

I GAVE THEM A SWORD AND THEY STUCK IT IN

178 "I gave them a sword and they stuck it in": David Frost, television interview with Richard Nixon, May 19, 1977.

179 "I was spread-eagled against the wall": John Dean, *Blind Ambition*, 357.

179 "[It] is an American tragedy": Gerald Ford, "Address to the Nation," September 8, 1974.

179 "The pardon violated the principle": James Cannon, "All the President's Witnesses," *Washington Post*, December 25, 1994.

180 "The son of a bitch pardoned": Farrell, *Richard Nixon*, 536.

180 "He drew up a secret plan": Drew, *Washington Journal*, 417.

180–81 "Well, when the president does it . . . I'd have done the same thing": David Frost, television interview with Richard Nixon, May 19, 1977.

181–82 "What do you know . . . I thought he was a crook": Private conversation with Andrea Balis, April 23, 1994.

EPILOGUE

185 "The Watergate affair . . . marked two national crises": Archibald Cox, "Watergate and the United States Constitution," *British Journal of Law and Society* 2, no. 1 (1975).

185 "What starts the process, really, are the laughs": Farrell, *Richard Nixon*, 535.

WHERE THEY ARE NOW: PEOPLE WHO WENT TO JAIL

189 "It could have been worse . . .": Katherine Winton Evans, "Washington's Other Martha," *Washington Post*, June 17, 1979.

190 "If they haven't changed . . .": Douglas Martin, Jeb Magruder obituary, *New York Times*, May 6, 2014.

PHOTO CREDITS

BIBLIOGRAPHY

Adler, Bill. *The Wit and Humor of Richard Nixon*. New York: Popular Library, 1969.

Archer, Jules. *Watergate: A Story of Richard Nixon and the Shocking 1972 Scandal*. 1975; repr. New York: Sky Pony Press, 2015, with foreword by Roger Stone.

Ben-Veniste, Richard, and George Frampton Jr. *Stonewall: The Legal Case Against the Watergate Conspirators*. New York: Touchstone, 1978.

Bernstein, Carl, and Bob Woodward. *All the President's Men*. 1974; 40th anniversary ed., New York: Simon & Schuster, 2014.

Black, Conrad. *Richard M. Nixon: A Life in Full*. New York: Public Affairs, 2007.

Breslin, Jimmy. *How the Good Guys Finally Won: Notes from an Impeachment Summer*. New York: Viking Press, 1975.

Brinkley, David, and Nichter, Luke, eds. *The Nixon Tapes: 1971–1972*. New York: Houghton Mifflin Harcourt, 2014.

———. *The Nixon Tapes: 1973*. New York: Houghton Mifflin Harcourt, 2015.

Brodie, Fawn W. *Richard Nixon: The Shaping of His Character*. New York: W. W. Norton, 1981.

Buchanan, Patrick J. *The Greatest Comeback: How Richard Nixon Rose from Defeat to Create the New Majority*. New York: Crown, 2014.

Colson, Charles W. *Born Again: What Really Happened to the White House Hatchet Man*. Old Tappan, NJ: Chosen Books, 1976.

Crowley, Monica. *Nixon in Winter: His Final Revelations about Diplomacy, Watergate, and Life out of the Arena*. New York: Random House, 1998.

———. *Nixon Off the Record: His Candid Commentary of People and Politics*. New York: Random House, 1996.

Dash, Samuel. *Chief Counsel: Inside the Ervin Committee—The Untold Story of Watergate*. New York: Random House, 1976.

Dean, John W. *Blind Ambition: The White House Years*. New York: Simon & Schuster, 1976.

————. *Lost Honor: The Rest of the Story*. Los Angeles: Stratford Press, 1982.

————. *The Nixon Defense: What He Knew and When He Knew It*. New York: Viking, 2014.

Dean, Maureen, with Hays Gorey. *"Mo": A Woman's View of Watergate*. New York: Simon & Schuster, 1975.

Doyle, James. *Not Above the Law: The Battle of Watergate Prosecutors Cox and Jaworski*. New York: Morrow, 1977.

Drew, Elizabeth. *Richard M. Nixon*. The American Presidents Series. New York: Times Books, 2008.

————. *Washington Journal: The Events of 1973–1974*. New York: Vintage, 1976.

Dudley, William, ed. *Watergate*. Examining Issues Through Political Cartoons. Farmington Hills, MI: Greenhaven Press, 2002.

Edmondson, Madeleine, and Alden Duer Cohen. *The Women of Watergate*. New York: Stein & Day, 1975.

Ehrlichman, John. *Witness to Power: The Nixon Years*. New York: Simon & Schuster, 1982.

Eisenhower, Julie Nixon. *Pat Nixon: The Untold Story*. New York: Simon & Schuster, 1986.

Ellsberg, Daniel. *Secrets: A Memoir of Vietnam and the Pentagon Papers*. New York: Penguin, 2003.

Emery, Fred. *Watergate: The Corruption of American Politics and the Fall of Richard Nixon*. New York: Touchstone, 1994.

Ervin, Sam J., Jr. *Humor of a Country Lawyer*. Chapel Hill: University of North Carolina Press, 1983.

————. *The Whole Truth: The Watergate Conspiracy*. New York: Random House, 1980.

Evans, Rowland, and Robert Novak. *Nixon in the White House*. New York: Random House, 1971.

Farrell, John. *Richard Nixon: The Life*. New York: Doubleday, 2017.

Frick, Daniel. *Reinventing Nixon: A Cultural History of an American Obsession*. Lawrence: University of Kansas Press, 2008.

Frost, David. *Frost/Nixon: Behind the Scenes of the Nixon Interviews*. New York: HarperCollins, 2007.

Genovese, Michael A. *The Watergate Crisis*. Westport, CT: Greenwood Press, 1999.

Gray, L. Patrick, III, with Ed Gray and Michael Prichard. *In Nixon's Web: A Year in the Crosshairs of Watergate*. New York: Times Books, 2010.

Haldeman, H. R. *The Haldeman Diaries*. New York: G. P. Putnam's Sons, 1994.

————, and Joseph DiMona. *The Ends of Power*. New York: Dell, 1978.

Hughes, Ken. *Fatal Politics: The Nixon Tapes, the Vietnam War, and the Casualties of Reelection*. Charlottesville: University of Virginia Press, 2015.

Hunt, E. Howard, with Greg Aunapu. *American Spy: My Secret History in the CIA, Watergate, and Beyond*. New York: John Wiley & Sons, 2007.

Hunt, St. John. *Dorothy, "An Amoral and Dangerous Woman": The Murder of E. Howard Hunt's Wife—Watergate's Darkest Secret*. Walterville, OR: Trine Day, 2014.

Jaworski, Leon. *The Right and the Power: The Prosecution of Watergate*. New York: Reader's Digest Press, 1976.

Knappman, Edward W., ed. *Watergate and the White House*, Vols. 1–3. New York: Facts on File, 1973–1974.

Kutler, Stanley, ed. *Abuse of Power: The New Nixon Tapes*. New York: Free Press, 1997.

————. *The Wars of Watergate: The Last Crisis of Richard Nixon*. New York: Knopf, 1990.

Lang, Gladys Engel, and Kurt Lang. *The Battle for Public Opinion: The President, the Press, and the Polls During Watergate*. New York: Columbia University Press, 1983.

Liddy, G. Gordon. *Will: The Autobiography of G. Gordon Liddy*. New York: St. Martin's Press, 1980.

Lukas, J. Anthony. *Nightmare: The Underside of the Nixon Years*. New York: Viking, 1976.

Magruder, Jeb Stuart. *An American Life: One Man's Road to Watergate*. New York: Atheneum, 1974.

Mallon, Thomas. *Watergate: A Novel*. New York: Pantheon, 2012.

Mankiewicz, Frank. *U.S. v. Richard M. Nixon: The Final Crisis*. New York: Quadrangle/The New York Times Book Company, 1975.

McCarthy, Mary. *The Mask of State: Watergate Portraits*. New York: Harcourt Brace Jovanovich, 1974.

McCord, James W., Jr. *A Piece of Tape: The Watergate Story—Fact and Fiction*. Rockville, MD: Washington Media Services, 1974.

Nixon, Richard. *RN: The Memoirs of Richard Nixon*. New York: Touchstone, 1978.

———. *Six Crises*. New York: Touchstone, 1962.

Osborne, John. *The Last Nixon Watch*. Washington, D.C.: New Republic Book Company, 1975.

Perlstein, Rick. *Nixonland: The Rise of a President and the Fracturing of America*. Scribner, 2008.

Reeves, Richard. *President Nixon: Alone in the White House*. New York: Touchstone, 2001.

Richardson, Elliot. *Reflections of a Radical Moderate*. New York: Pantheon, 1996.

Rodota, Joseph. *The Watergate: Inside America's Most Infamous Address*. New York: HarperCollins, 2018.

Rosen, James. *The Strong Man: John Mitchell and the Secrets of Watergate*. New York: Doubleday, 2012.

Safire, William. *Before the Fall: An Insider View of the Pre-Watergate White House*. New York: Doubleday, 1975.

Sheinkin, Steve. *Most Dangerous: Daniel Ellsberg and the Secret History of the Vietnam War*. New York: Roaring Brook Press, 2015.

Sirica, John J. *To Set the Record Straight: The Break-In, the Tapes, the Conspirators, the Pardon*. New York: Norton, 1979.

Stone, Roger, with Mike Colapietro. *Nixon's Secrets: The Rise, Fall, and Untold Truth About the President, Watergate, and the Pardon*. New York: Skyhorse Publishing, 2014.

Strober, Deborah Hart, and Gerald Strober. *The Nixon Presidency: An Oral History of the Era*. Washington, D.C.: Brassey's, 2003.

Swift, Will. *Pat and Dick: The Nixons, an Intimate Portrait of a Marriage*. New York: Simon & Schuster, 2014.

Thomas, Evan. *Being Nixon: A Man Divided*. New York: Random House, 2015.

Thompson, Fred. *At That Point in Time: The Inside Story of the Watergate Committee*. New York: Quadrangle/The New York Times Book Company, 1975.

Thompson, Hunter S. *The Great Shark Hunt: Strange Tales from a Strange Time*. New York: Summit Books, 1979.

Ulasewicz, Tony, with Stuart A. McKeever. *The President's Private Eye: The Journey of Detective Tony U. from N.Y.P.D. to the Nixon White House*. Westport, CT: MASCAM Publishing Company, 1990.

Weiner, Tim. *One Man Against the World: The Tragedy of Richard Nixon*. New York: Henry Holt, 2015.

White, Theodore. *Breach of Faith: The Fall of Richard Nixon*. New York: Atheneum, 1975.

Wicker, Tom. *One of Us: Richard Nixon and the American Dream*. New York: Random House, 1991.

Wills, Garry. *Nixon Agonistes: The Crisis of the Self-Made Man*. Boston: Houghton Mifflin, 1969.

Witcover, Jules. *The Resurrection of Richard Nixon*. New York: G. P. Putnam's Sons, 1970.

Woodward, Bob. *The Secret Man: The Story of Watergate's Deep Throat*. New York: Simon & Schuster, 2005.

Woodward, Bob. *Fear: Trump in the White House*. New York: Simon & Schuster, 2018.

———, and Carl Bernstein. *The Final Days*. New York: Simon & Schuster, 1976.

ACKNOWLEDGMENTS

Collaboration, while not always smooth, is very special. We have been very lucky, not only with each other but with everyone who helped us.

We have many people to thank.

Jodi Reamer, our agent at Writers House, believed in this book from the beginning and understood immediately why it was important to tell this history to the young people who didn't live through it.

Emily Feinberg, our editor at Roaring Brook, instantly connected with both the book and with us, and her steadfast support, good humor, and snacks have been a rock.

Heroic copyediting was done at Roaring Brook by Janet Renard and Nancy Elgin, and by our own private copyediting team, Linda Broessel and Erica Levy-Ringel.

We want to thank Tim Foley for his lively illustrations and April Ward for her brilliant design. Their skills brought this history to life.

We are deeply grateful to the Department of History at John Jay College of Criminal Justice, where Professor Balis teaches, for housing us and for endless patience with our sometimes loud collaborative efforts.

To the students at John Jay College who reminded us daily of why this work is valuable, frequently laughed at our jokes, and asked us the most important question: "Did this really happen?"

We want to thank Professor Itai Sneh for reading the manuscript for accuracy and balance, and Professor Blanche Wiesen Cook for her insights into the political context of the period.

We thank the research staff of the Lloyd Sealy Library at John Jay College for their patience and their sympathetic assistance with our searches, and for never commenting on the size of our fines for late returns.

We also relied on public collections of documents, the best sources of which were the Nixon Library, the Library of Congress, and the Miller Center at the University of Virginia.

We are indebted to our friends and fellow authors Robie Harris, Theodora Skipitares, Susan Kuklin, Dana Alison Levy, Patty Lakin, Roxane Orgill, and Lucy Frank for carefully reading, listening to us complain, and cheerfully providing useful criticism, even when we sometimes ignored it.

To our families, Marshall Marcovitz and George Harris, Jesse Balis Harris, Sophie Balis Harris, and Caitlin Millat, for not only putting up with us while we were writing but also encouraging us to continue, reading endless drafts, and laughing, each time, at all those Watergate jokes.

It takes a village.

INDEX